The Marriage of Margery Paston

Boss from Norwich Cathedral cloister

The Marriage of Margery Paston

A true story

Susan Curran

Lasse
Press

First published 2013
by the Lasse Press
2 St Giles Terrace, Norwich NR2 1NS, UK
www.lassepress.com
lassepress@gmail.com

Also published in electronic versions

ISBN-13: 978-0-9568758-4-6

Typeset in Frutiger, Garamond and Stone Sans by
Curran Publishing Services Ltd, Norwich, UK

Manufactured in the UK by LPPS Ltd, Wellingborough, Northants NN8 3PJ

It seems a thousand years ago since I spoke with you, and I had rather be with you than possess all the goods in the world.

Richard Calle to Margery Paston, 1469

... if she had been good, whatsoever she had been it would not have been as it is, for if he [Richard Calle] were dead at this hour she should never be in my heart as she was.

Margaret Paston (Margery's mother), 1469

For Paul

Contents

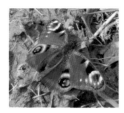

Maps

Genealogies

East Anglia in the fifteenth century, showing places mentioned in the book

Church of St Mary, Saxlingham Nethergate, Norfolk

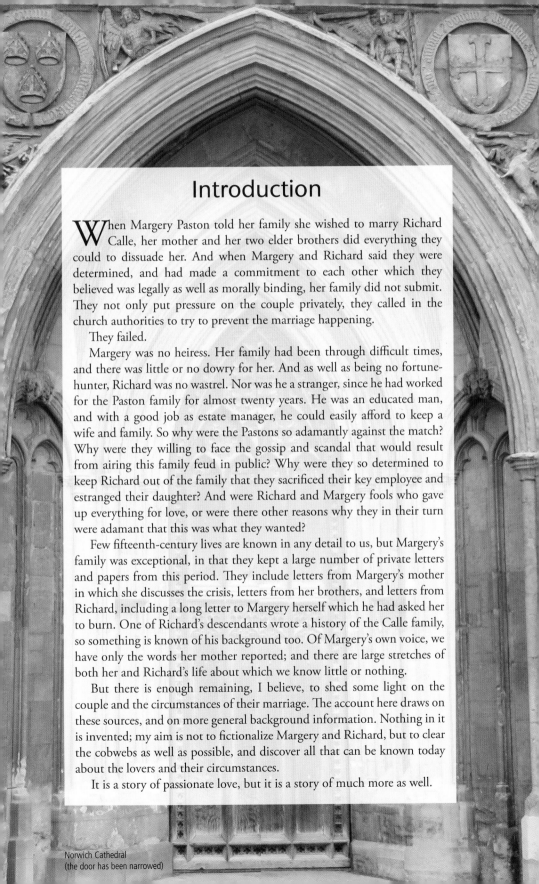

Introduction

When Margery Paston told her family she wished to marry Richard Calle, her mother and her two elder brothers did everything they could to dissuade her. And when Margery and Richard said they were determined, and had made a commitment to each other which they believed was legally as well as morally binding, her family did not submit. They not only put pressure on the couple privately, they called in the church authorities to try to prevent the marriage happening.

They failed.

Margery was no heiress. Her family had been through difficult times, and there was little or no dowry for her. And as well as being no fortune-hunter, Richard was no wastrel. Nor was he a stranger, since he had worked for the Paston family for almost twenty years. He was an educated man, and with a good job as estate manager, he could easily afford to keep a wife and family. So why were the Pastons so adamantly against the match? Why were they willing to face the gossip and scandal that would result from airing this family feud in public? Why were they so determined to keep Richard out of the family that they sacrificed their key employee and estranged their daughter? And were Richard and Margery fools who gave up everything for love, or were there other reasons why they in their turn were adamant that this was what they wanted?

Few fifteenth-century lives are known in any detail to us, but Margery's family was exceptional, in that they kept a large number of private letters and papers from this period. They include letters from Margery's mother in which she discusses the crisis, letters from her brothers, and letters from Richard, including a long letter to Margery herself which he had asked her to burn. One of Richard's descendants wrote a history of the Calle family, so something is known of his background too. Of Margery's own voice, we have only the words her mother reported; and there are large stretches of both her and Richard's life about which we know little or nothing.

But there is enough remaining, I believe, to shed some light on the couple and the circumstances of their marriage. The account here draws on these sources, and on more general background information. Nothing in it is invented; my aim is not to fictionalize Margery and Richard, but to clear the cobwebs as well as possible, and discover all that can be known today about the lovers and their circumstances.

It is a story of passionate love, but it is a story of much more as well.

Norwich Cathedral
(the door has been narrowed)

Church of St Mary Magdalene, Mulbarton, Norfolk

1
The heiress

Finding a husband for Margaret Mautby would never have been a problem. The only issue for her family was to choose among her competing suitors.

She was a healthy girl, bright and competent, but the main reason for her desirability on the marriage market was of course financial. In fifteenth-century England, marriages among the gentry were almost always based on money. Margaret's father had died when she was eleven, so she would remain his only child and heir to all his estates. Her mother had remarried after his death, but by the time Margaret was in her early teens she had had no more children, so her mother's estate would probably all pass to her too in due course.

The Mautbys and the Berneys (Margaret's mother's family) were solidly respectable people. They played their part in Norfolk society – their lands were in the middle and south-east of the county – but were not particularly prominent, nor did they show any real signs of ambition. No one seems to have aspired to make a brilliant marriage for Margaret; they were not interested in pushing her into the aristocracy. They looked, rather, to find her a husband among families not dissimilar to her own: good gentry folk, living near enough to hand that Margaret might stay in close touch with her mother.

The man who became Margaret's husband was John Paston, the eldest son of Judge William Paston. He fitted this pattern well. The Pastons were also a Norfolk family (though from farther to the north of the county), probably a little richer than Margaret's relatives, and John was a well-educated young man, a year or so older than Margaret herself. Judge Paston was considerably more forceful than any of Margaret's relatives, so he drove a tough bargain, but it was a fair one, as was necessary when she had plenty of other suitors. As part of the marriage agreement the Pastons settled the estate of Gresham in north Norfolk on the couple.[1] It was good farmland, some of it probably farmed direct and the rest put out to tenants, as was the norm in that region, and it also boasted a strong stone castle.

Details are scarce about the couple's life in the early years of their marriage, but it is likely that Margaret spent much of her time in Norwich, as did the elder Pastons and most of the other affluent Norfolk gentry, and some of it living in the castle at Gresham, or staying with her in-laws on the other Paston estates. She would have made it a priority to visit and be visited by her mother as well. Hers was a close family, and she seems to have been on happy terms with her stepfather. Probably at least one of her children was born in her mother and stepfather's house.[2]

Her husband's pattern was rather different. Judge Paston was educating all his sons in the law: a sensible enough plan, though some might have thought it lacking in balance. There were no aspiring clergy or men at arms among them, and in time they might be falling over each other's feet. But the law had served their father well, and he clearly believed that a good grounding in it would enable his sons both to manage their own estates effectively, and to earn money providing advice and services to the gentry and nobility, as he had done himself.

In pursuit of this ambition John spent much of his time in London at the Inner Temple. Margaret seems to have followed him there rarely, if at all: her role was to manage affairs in Norfolk. This too was a common pattern, and it does not imply there was a falling-out between the pair. On the contrary, these were probably happy years for them. It is not easy for any young girl to join a new family, but Margaret seems to have kept on reasonable terms with her parents-in-law, and on good terms with her husband.

She must have delighted both families by giving birth to two sons in fairly quick succession.[3] Improbably, she and her husband named them both John, most likely not after their father, but after influential godparents or connections. (John had been her father's name, and it was also, for instance, the name of her extremely rich relative, Sir John Fastolf.) But 1444, the year when John III (as I shall call him, to distinguish him from his elder brother and his father) was born, was also the year in which Judge Paston sickened and died.

This led to a major downturn in Margaret and John's lives.

Judge Paston was sixty-six when he died. His wife Agnes was probably in her early forties, and their children ranged in age from John – then twenty-three – down to Clement, aged two, like his nephew John II. It was not a sudden death, since the judge had been sick for some months beforehand, but it was one that was not handled well.

From his family's viewpoint his death came too soon, or perhaps rather his marriage had come too late. His sons were not old enough to take over his business, and the family was weakened as a result. It was a major problem too that the judge had not finalized his will, or left his family with an unambiguous sense of his intentions.[4] This was probably not – or not only – because like many powerful men, he had found it hard to envisage a world in which he no longer existed. It was also because it was not easy to see what could best be done. Although the family had plenty of land, much of it would remain in his widow's hands for the rest of her life. That could well be another forty years, a period during which her children needed to be provided for from the remainder. (Agnes never showed any inclination to provide for her offspring out of her own portion.) That remainder would not go to a sole heir, as had the Mautby lands, but would have to be shared among four sons and a daughter. In addition, the judge wanted to see a grand memorial made to his own memory: he had achieved much in his life, and he did not want to see it forgotten.

Margaret's young husband had not inherited his father's drive and fierce intellect, as she had no doubt realized by then. He made up for their lack, however, with a wily cunning of his own. When his father suggested that many of the family's smaller estates should be granted to his siblings, he fought this bitterly, because he believed, with some reason, that he would then be left with too little to maintain his position in life. And when these issues were still not resolved on the judge's death, he took action on his own behalf. He abstracted the deeds to the disputed estates from his mother's possession, and he also spirited out of Norwich priory, where they had been left for safe-keeping, all of his father's money and valuables.[5]

His mother was outraged, and so were his brothers. The price of securing the disputed lands and money was a rift between them that to a large extent would never be healed.

If the family made efforts to keep the scandal private, they could never have been entirely successful. Judge Paston had named two colleagues, John Damme and John Bacton, as executors of his (provisional) will, and it was inevitable that they would learn what had happened. Norfolk society was small and close-knit, and its links spread out into the rest of the country. Those men (and women) who had already noted that young John Paston had neither the experience nor the personality to replace his father also took note of this family feud, and of the impact it would have on John's backing and resources.

The wolves circled.

Margaret was now to learn (if she had not already) quite how different the Pastons were

Mautby, Norfolk

from the Mautbys and Berneys. Those were long-established families, who had built up their holdings of land and other possessions over generations. The Pastons were not. Their background was so obscure that many men believed Judge Paston's near ancestors had been bondmen: men tied to the land and a master, and not entitled to own property of their own. This was an era in which the last vestiges of the old feudal system were dying, and even in the 1440s such prohibitions would have been hard to enforce. But it was also an era when people's sense of their position in life, and that of others, was of great importance to them. To claim that someone was born into bondage was a slur, something that could only damage the judge's family.

What was more, it was almost certainly true.

An awareness of that, perhaps, lay behind Agnes Paston's determination to ensure that she kept much of the family land firmly in her own hands. In her own eyes (and those of many others) it would have been safer there. She was a Berry, son of a knight; no one questioned her parentage as they questioned her late husband's. Like her eldest son, she had grabbed as much as she could for herself, and she clung bitterly on to it.

Ownership of land has always been an emotive subject. In the late middle ages it was also a complex one. No title to land was absolute; in the last resort, everything was held from the king. The king could (and kings did) both confiscate and grant land holdings. There was no central registry of holdings, and although there were deeds that purported to show a right to possession, everyone knew that such papers could be (and often were) forged. There was much security in the long-established ownership of family estates, like those at Mautby that Margaret had inherited. But when someone paid money for land – land that had previously belonged to some other family – there was far less security associated, however much care they took over the documentation, however certain the title to that land might appear to be. There were always those among the tenants and cottagers who thought of the land on which they lived as, say, Bacon family land, even if the title to it was now in the hands of, say, the Paston family.

In the months and years after Judge Paston's death, a clutch of claimants to his estates crawled out of their wormholes and burrows. They were betting that what the judge had assembled so rapidly might prove to be disassemblable almost as quickly. They knew that questions raised over one estate would tend to give credence to questions raised over another one. They knew that by no means everyone in Norfolk (and beyond) had appreciated the judge's rapid rise in society, and that more than a few people would not regret it were his family to fall back to a lower level.

The judge and his wife had made their main home at Oxnead, not far from Gresham, where they had invested heavily in building a fine new house. A friar appeared, with claims that the Oxnead estate had been wrongly acquired, and its true title rested with him.[6] The friar did not produce incontrovertible evidence of his claim, but some believed it even so. And when young Lord Moleyns announced that the estate at Gresham that the Pastons claimed was in fact the property of his own family, people believed him too.

Moleyns was a man at arms. The king had need of such men, and appreciated their need for sufficient lands (and income from them) to maintain their position. Moleyns was supported by some of the great lords of East Anglia, among whom at the time the duke of Suffolk – probably the most powerful man in England – was pre-eminent. He was married to a descendant of the Bacon family that had owned Gresham for generations, and built the fine stone castle there. True, after squabbles among the Bacon and Moleyns heirs the family had lost their land at Gresham: but it was still the bones of the Bacons that rested in Gresham churchyard. No Paston bones rested there, and many men living on the Gresham estate would have seen little or nothing of either Judge Paston or his son. Perhaps it was not such a wonder that men were slow to dismiss Lord Moleyns' claim, and to assure John Paston and his wife that the land that had been settled on them was indisputably theirs.

This was bad enough, but in 1448 things took a still more serious turn for the worse. Lord

Moleyns sent a contingent of men to Gresham, at a time when the Pastons were not in residence. They broke into and occupied the castle, and claimed the estate in their master's name.

Church of
St Peter and St Paul,
Bardwell, Suffolk

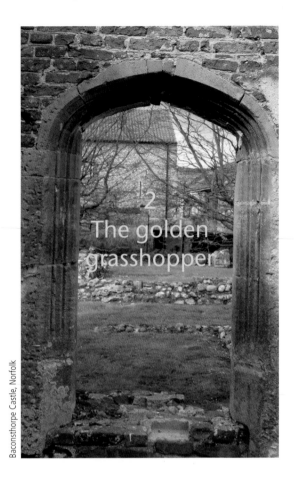

Baconsthorpe Castle, Norfolk

2
The golden
grasshopper

In October 1448 Margaret Paston came to Gresham.[1] She came without her husband, though there is no reason to think they had quarrelled, either about her coming there, or about his failing to do so. Margaret seems to have been a loyal and dutiful wife, and though she was very capable of expressing her own opinions, and acting upon them, she would not have done anything her husband forbade her to do.

She brought her maidservant Kate with her, and a group of men, perhaps a dozen of them. They did not include any of her husband's brothers, but that was no wonder: William was studying in London, Edmund in Cambridge, and Clement was still a small child, so none of them were realistically available to accompany her. John had no uncles or other close male relatives who might have supported her. (Agnes Paston might just have qualified as a support, but she did not come.) Margaret had uncles herself, but at this stage she had perhaps not asked for help from them, or from the other men of the county with whom her in-laws had regular dealings, such as Judge Paston's executors. Her stepfather had died a couple of years earlier, and she had not asked her mother to come to Gresham.

The man in her escort to whom she was closest, and on whom she relied the most, was James Gloys, a priest who had been acting for some time as chaplain to the Paston family. He now served Margaret as well as Agnes, and she clearly rated him highly. Gloys was no weedy cleric, he was capable of wielding a dagger.[2] Other men in the group would also have been trained with weapons. Most likely some of them were established servants of the family, and others were men she had hired to provide security for this venture. There was a truce in the long war with the French, and many men with no pay to claim in France had come back to England to look for work, so it was easy to pick up such men when they were needed.

The village of Gresham is set on what counts for high land in Norfolk, a county with no mountains and few large hills. It is the church that crests the hill, as is common in these parts, and the castle – scant ruins now, but in 1448 a solid square stone building, with round towers at each corner, set in a moat – lies half a mile away on lower ground. There was a windmill high up (as it must be) close by the church, and a watermill down by Gut Beck, the little stream – it could hardly be called a river, though it was just about navigable[3] – that fed the moat.

This geography implies that the village land had once been divided into at least two separate manors, or estates, with a manor house for one of them near to the church, and the castle on the site of the house for a second manor. But long before this time they had become one large holding, and since the castle that Sir Edmund Bacon had crenellated a century and a half before was the obvious place for the lord to live, the old manor house had lost its purpose. It seems not to have been lived in at all as a rule, something that was not unusual in those days, since the population of England was still barely half what it had been a century earlier, before the first of the great plagues that had ravaged the country. It was a wood-framed house, probably sturdy but dilapidated and dirty, with a thatched roof.

Since Lord Moleyns' men were in the castle, Margaret must have set her path to the manor house.[4] She would have put her servants to sweeping the place out, lighting a fire to warm it, then once the carts had been unloaded, and the bread and meat was in the pantry, the barrels of ale in the buttery, the best bed set ready for her in the solar, they would have been given orders to strengthen the house as best they could. Margaret seems to have been receiving reasonably regular updates on the situation at Gresham, so she knew that Moleyns' men were headed by one Partridge. It stood to reason that once he learned she had moved in, she was likely to receive a visit from him and his men.

Although she would have known Gresham well, it must have been strange to be in this old house and not behind the stone walls of the castle, to have no drawbridge to pull up after her, to look out onto the windmill and the old flint round tower of All Saints and not the watermill and the low meadows. And though she was a feisty woman, never one to shirk what she saw as her duty, she must have been uneasy about her situation. There was a small chance that once he learned the Pastons had taken steps to reclaim Gresham, Lord Moleyns would withdraw his men and leave it to them, but it was not a possibility a wise man would have bet on. If Moleyns chose to push it to a confrontation, then realistically Margaret was not likely to win. Moleyns was the richer and better connected of the two claimants: he could outgun and outbribe the Pastons very easily.

What might she achieve, then? Perhaps she saw it most of all as a necessary statement of intent, to back up the lawsuits on which her husband was spending his time, and in which he was placing his trust. She must have been very aware of how much clout the Paston family had lost in the years since the judge's death. They had to make efforts to reverse the situation, even if the odds were against them. Taking a stand at Gresham would remind other men of the rightness of their case, and it might also serve to deter the friar who had been circling around Oxnead, and other men and women who had lodged claims to other of the family's lands. Anyway, Gresham was personally very important to her. It was not just one of the family estates, it was the estate that sat at the core of her and John's own holdings.

Father Gloys probably left quite quickly, although he returned to check on Margaret and offer his support from time to time. He knew better than to neglect Agnes Paston in favour of her daughter in law. Once he was gone, Margaret must have felt very alone. Perhaps she appreciated that John was needed in London, but she must have known too that it suited John to be in London. He was not the man to wave a sword in the face of a band of mercenaries. She was no complainer, though, and she kept any qualms she felt to herself.

Partridge probably visited quite quickly, and he and Margaret perhaps had words over the garden wall, with his men standing behind him, and hers behind her. There was no fight, yet. Margaret fortified herself by writing letters. There was a positive flurry of them over the next few weeks: from Partridge to Moleyns, from Margaret to John in London, and to her own family down in south-east Norfolk. She must have needed encouragement, and hoped for support. There is no indication that she got much of either.

Gresham was home to the legend of the grasshopper.[5] Generations before, it was said, the lady of the manor, out walking in the fields, had come across a baby boy, lying abandoned, but sheltered from harm by a giant golden grasshopper. She and her husband, who were childless, had adopted the boy, who grew up to be lord of the manor in his turn. The village's name echoed that story – grass ham, the village of the grass and the grasshoppers who lived in it. This was good farmland, fit for arable crops as well as the sheep that dominated the Norfolk economy, and there were thick woodlands too.

It had never been a town, or even a large village. There were perhaps little more than a dozen houses around the church, while the rest of the parish's population lived on scattered farms. Though a fair way from any city – it is about twenty-five miles due north of Norwich, on the road that leads through Aylsham – it was not remote or isolated: this was well-tended, thickly inhabited countryside. The sea was six or seven miles away, distant enough that there was no threat here from the pirates who plagued the coast in those times.

After the flurry of Margaret's moving in, the village might have seemed peaceful to a passer-by. But this was not so. Partridge and his men did not come armed to the old manor and try to drive her out, but they and the Pastons' men were fighting a quiet battle, farm by farm, cottage by cottage. A landowner drew his income from the crops on the land that was farmed direct, by the men he employed; from the rents of the lands he let out to tenants; and from dues owed to him by the manor's bondmen. All these people, from the humblest cottagers to the richest tenant farmers, had to be shown who their landlord was, and Partridge's men and Margaret Paston's men were both set on driving home this lesson.

Church of, St Mary Magdalene, Mulbarton, Norfolk

This was hard news for the tenants, who were visited by two groups of men, both set on taking dues from them, and both threatening action if they were not paid. (It was men who did this work as a rule, though on at least one occasion Kate carried out an errand the men refused to risk, and Margaret did not always limit herself to giving her servants a good push from within the walls of the manor house.) The usual first line of action in these circumstances was distraint, taking a man's goods in lieu of what he owed. Disputes over land titles were not uncommon, and nor was a simple failure to pay the rent due, so although it was a harsh remedy, distraint was not an unusual one. But the threat of it was often sufficient to get the rent paid: no man wanted to lose his cows and pigs. This time it was not enough. Margaret's men reported back to her that some of the tenants were refusing to pay, and she told them that in that case, the threat would have to be carried out.

Margaret's estate servants were hardened men, used to carrying out difficult and disagreeable assignments, but with the likelihood of interference from Lord Moleyns' men, distraining goods at Gresham was liable to be even more problematic than it usually was. Not only might their opponents intervene to prevent goods from being taken, they could take action in the courts. If it was argued that the Pastons did not have a valid title to Gresham, it followed that they did not have a right to claim rents, or to take goods in their stead. Distraint became theft: and charges of theft, if they were not answered (to a schedule that was not always apparent to the accused), could lead to a declaration of outlawry, and to the right to put a man to death.

Margaret would have been very well aware of this, so it is no wonder that she waited till Father Gloys returned before sending the men out to take the enforcement action. He led the party that went off to distrain a tenant called James Rockerson. When they returned some hours some hours later, they were winded and shaken. They had taken Rockerson's goods without difficulty, they reported to Margaret, but while they were driving the livestock away they had run into Partridge and a group of his men.

Partridge had made a great show of anger, and Father Gloys had given him insult for insult. They had stopped just short of blows. But Partridge had made it very clear that he felt the Paston men had stepped over a line, and he would defend it. If they distrained any more tenants, Lord Moleyns' men would come and take their animals back by force.

Most likely, Margaret and Gloys agreed, Partridge would come to the manor to make sure she heard his message at first hand. Margaret was determined not to back down to him. She had assembled some padded jackets and helmets, no substitute for plate armour, but decent protection for a man facing a dagger or a stave. She told her men to put them on that afternoon. So when a couple of visitors came riding up the hill to the manor, they were greeted by Margaret and her servants in their war gear.

The visitors were not Lord Moleyns' men. One was Margaret's uncle John Berney, and the other was the parson of Oxnead.[6] At the sight of the jackets and helmets, they turned white as geese.

John Berney was not a young man. Perhaps it would be as well, he suggested, if he headed straight back home.

As well for whom, Margaret might have asked? She needed help from her family, from men such as this one. She managed to persuade Berney to stay for supper, but he was clearly uneasy, and as soon as the meal was over he insisted on saddling up his horse and riding off. Supper was taken early those days, so even in November he could have ridden a few miles before nightfall. She begged him to find her help, send her some men who could better protect her. Moleyns might persist if he believed there was little more than Margaret and her husband set against him, but if she could persuade men of the county to stand shoulder to shoulder with them, surely he would be dissuaded. The judge had bought a valid title to Gresham, so there was no real substance to Moleyns' claim, it was all braggardy and force.

One of Margaret's servants told her he had learned that when Partridge's men had first come to Gresham, Berney had been not far off, but he had chosen not to go to the village and confront the invaders, but to turn back. This man clearly did not expect Berney to make good on his reluctantly given promise to come back soon with some substantial assistance. And he was right: Berney sent his man from Norwich a few days later, to say that his horse had kicked out and hit him on the hip, and he was too bruised to make the journey again.

That was a cheap lie. Gloys asked the parson of Oxnead when he saw him the following day, and was told he had seen Berney, who was perfectly fine.

So no help was likely to come from that direction. Margaret was continuing to write to her husband, and he too was continuing not to come to Gresham. She seems to have contacted some of the other men who had long been associated with the Pastons, and perhaps she did get a little assistance and encouragement from some of them.[7]

Down by the stream, Partridge and his troops were strengthening the defences of the castle. It hardly needed it: the strong stone walls, the round towers at each corner, the moat, were more than enough to ensure that two women and a dozen serving men would not storm the place. Margaret's men must have laughed to keep their spirits up as their rivals nailed bars crosswise over the doors, and built out little wickets from the towers so they could shoot at attackers with bows or handguns without exposing themselves to crossfire. Margaret wrote to her husband again, and managed to joke about it: they're sore afraid we'll come for them, she told him.[8]

She must have been increasingly aware, though, that at some point Partridge's men would come for her, and that when they did it would be no laughing matter. This standoff was costing both parties, and neither could maintain it for ever. There must have seemed to her no likelihood that Lord Moleyns would win any case in the lawcourts, so if he wanted Gresham, he would have to finish the job he had started, and take the place by force.

The Pastons claimed afterwards that they had kept money as well as goods at Gresham, but that might have been a lie: Margaret was surely not so stupid or so confident. She did her best to strengthen the defences of the old house, and she did so because she expected an attack. Her men were maybe not sure of their skill with guns, so she wrote to ask John to find her some crossbows and windlasses to draw them with, and quarrels, the darts to shoot from them. The men might have preferred longbows, but the old manor house was no castle: its windows were low to the ground, and a man with a six-foot longbow could not have shot from them. Two or three poleaxes would be useful too, she wrote, and as many more padded jackets as he could lay his hands on. These were not items that John can have had much need for at the Inns of Court, but he was doing some legal work for Sir John Fastolf, an old soldier recently back from France, and she reckoned Fastolf's men would have a good arsenal that he could call on.

The winter wore on, and up at the top of the hill Margaret and her servants shivered through it. Probably her husband came to Gresham that Christmas; he usually spent the feast with his family, however much he stayed away the rest of the year. He left again afterwards, and quite likely he left his wife pregnant. If she begged him to stay with her, there is no indication remaining of it. Perhaps she did not. Perhaps she believed, as he did, that the work he was doing in London to try to get the estate restored was more important than anything that could be achieved on the ground at Gresham.

Lord Moleyns did not come.

However, he continued to build up his forces. By January it was said he had a thousand men in and around Gresham. Realistically he would not have needed so many men to confront Margaret's tiny band, even if all the tenants had stood by her side. Perhaps it was not even entirely his choice that so many men had assembled. Most of the soldiers who had left France had no proper occupation, and were hard pushed to make a living. It would have been no wonder if, hearing that Moleyns was assembling men at Gresham, they had chosen to head along to join them. Even if Moleyns did not pay them, the affair was likely to end with a sacking, an action they knew all too well. The profits of the raid would compensate them for their time.

There were many more men than could have been billeted in the castle, so most of them must have camped out in the meadow. Perhaps a contingent stayed in Baconsthorpe nearby, where one of the duke of Suffolk's men of business, a known supporter of Moleyns, had a castle. They had a rough livery, bands of white cloth that they tied round their jackets. Some of them had plate armour, and had fastened the white bands over their steel breastplates. They had bows and arrows, firepans, long hook-ended sticks for pulling off thatch, ladders and picks for breaking down walls.

It must have been a scary situation for Margaret and her men. A thousand men, barely controlled, used to causing mayhem, and spoiling for a fight: this was no longer simply about the rights of a land title, it was about brute force and survival. These men would not go until they had their rewards. Even the duke of Suffolk himself could not have dispersed them peacefully.

Every day, Margaret have woken to wonder if this would be the day the guns fired on the manor house.

Still she stayed in Gresham, and kept her servants there with her. It was not till 28 January 1449, when the standoff had persisted for pushing four months, that Partridge gave his men the order.

A thousand men, tramping up the hill and into Gresham village. Guns, those new-fangled lethal contraptions that these men actually seemed to know how to use. Crossbows and longbows, more familiar but no less dangerous: everyone knew a well-aimed arrow could kill a man outright. Enough men and equipment to turn the house to kindling in an afternoon.

Margaret and her men would have been fools to fight. All that was left to her now was to stand firm and refuse to run, to drive home the message as firmly as she might that she was convinced of the rightness of her cause. Perhaps the men of Norfolk who

All Saints Church, Gresham, Norfolk

had failed to come and stand by her would at least feel some sympathy if she was turned out of her house by force.

Margaret's servants let the men into the house, to the hall where she was waiting for them. Partridge led the way. Your husband's not here, he asked her? No, John was not there. Perhaps as well, Partridge said. Orders are, if he's here we are to kill him. [9]

Whose orders? Lord Moleyns'? The court's? Perhaps they had cobbled together some kind of justification for this, but just as likely not. Margaret believed it, though.

At least their orders were not to kill her. The white-banded men picked her up and carried her out of the house and into the road. Her servants clustered round her. And they watched, powerless, indignant, despairing, as Partridge's army carted off to the castle the chests and crates that held the family's possessions.

They ripped the mattresses to pieces, scattering the straw about the yard. They tossed out barrels of ale, some of them still half full, and the yard filled with the sour smell of it seeping into the earth. This was vandalism and thievery, outright damned thievery: whatever the rights and wrongs of the title to the manor, the Pastons' sheets and silver did not belong to Lord Moleyns. Then they chopped through the posts of the house, yanked at the walling and the thatch, till it came tumbling down, a sorry wreck.

That was the end of Margaret Paston's life in Gresham.

Church of St Peter, North Barningham, Norfolk

All Saints Church, Gresham, Norfolk

3
Boar spears
and swords

In 1449 and 1450 King Henry VI's holdings in France unravelled with alarming speed, and his administration in England unravelled almost as fast. The long war with France had been set at stalemate for a generation, since the death of Henry V in 1422. The English house of Lancaster was not strong enough to complete its conquest, and its rival, the house of Valois, was so weak and divided that it could not drive the English back from the tidemark that Henry V had established. The English did not become significantly less strong in the late 1440s, but the Valois became significantly more so. When they finally made a push, they found nothing in place to resist their surge forwards.

The trickle of English men at arms who had returned to England during the truce (which was broken in early 1449) became a flood as the Lancastrians lost control of town after town, castle after castle in northern and central France. Angry, disillusioned and broke, they fomented unrest across the country, and nowhere more than in the eastern counties where they landed. They killed the duke of Suffolk, and other of the king's coun-sellors whom they blamed for the disaster, and the government was not strong enough to bring the murderers to justice. One Jack Cade started an uprising which looked for a time as if it might become a revolution, and men of substance as well as those with less to lose were among those who supported him.

The Pastons were not. John Paston was more concerned to protect his own position than to fight for wider causes. And he needed to do so, because although there was sympathy for him and Margaret after the attack on Gresham, this was not a time when that sympathy translated into immediate firm action against Lord Moleyns and his men.

Any suggestion that Lord Moleyns was simply taking reasonable action to claim what was his evaporated with the behaviour of his men after they had ousted Margaret. Many of the men who had been at Gresham for the storming of the manor dispersed afterwards – taking the Pastons' goods with them – but others stayed on the estate, and proceeded to terrorize the farmers and their servants.[1] They not only ransacked the farmhouses, they went in search of the men and women who had fled from them, hacking through their haystacks and the piles of fodder in their barns with boar spears and swords. Those they caught they beat so brutally that some were left for dead. They coerced men and women to lay complaints against the Pastons at the manor court – which they ran themselves – and found against the Pastons every time. They turned their staves and hooks on the castle, and reduced that too to little more than a ruin. By the time they moved on, Gresham was a wasteland, as empty and ravished as the lands of northern France.

It was around this time – perhaps in 1450 – that Margaret Paston gave birth to her first daughter.[2] She gave her a name from her own family, not a Paston one: the child was called Margery after her mother.

The first years of young Margery's life must have been frightening ones for her parents, and indeed for almost everyone in Norfolk. Gangs of robbers and vandals all but ruled the county for a while.[3] They set upon a couple of the bishop of Norwich's servants while they were kneeling at the mass, and came close to killing them before men managed to come to their rescue. Men armed with swords and daggers attacked John Paston, who was with two of his servants at the door to the cathedral, on the Monday before Easter in 1452. The grabbed his arms and pulled them behind his back, and he feared for a moment that he would be murdered. (Again, other men came to his rescue, and managed to drive the attackers off.) They hit one of the servants over the head with a sword, and polluted the cathedral sanctuary with the blood they spilled. They shot arrows at Philip Berney, another of Margaret's uncles, while he was riding through Thorp Wood outside Norwich with his man, killing his horse, and broke a bow over Berney's head. Their aim, it seemed, was to grab a manor that the Berney family had owned for generations at Rocklandtofts. Poor Philip Berney had no one else to come to his rescue: he died of his wounds.[4] Many others suffered too, with goods stolen, attacks made, lands devastated.

But slowly the tide turned. Just as men who feared revolution more than its alternative banded together to destroy Cade's rebellion, so men in Norfolk banded together to support John Paston, and the many other men across the country who had suffered. It was a help to them that the duke of Suffolk was dead, and his heir a small child. Suffolk

had never been a friend to Judge Paston or his sons, while his death brought more weight to the dukes of Norfolk and Oxford, the other great landowners of the region, and both of these were better disposed. Lord Moleyns did not come to Gresham to try to restore order following the chaos that had been inflicted in his name; instead he went to France, with the small and inadequate army that was raised to try to arrest the haemorrhaging. He was captured in 1453 at the battle of Castillon (the final disastrous action of the Hundred Years' War), and in his absence the forces of law prevailed: the Pastons were confirmed in the title to their estate.

They were never compensated for the damage and the thefts, however. And more had been lost than barrels of beer and chests of linen: a sense of security had gone from the country. Through Margery's lifetime, it would never entirely return.

Church of St Lawrence, Little Waldingfield, Suffolk

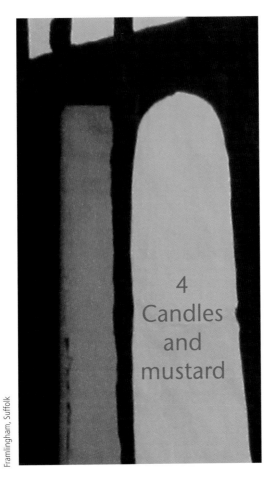

Framlingham, Suffolk

4
Candles
and
mustard

In these restless and unnerving times, men would have turned to the king to restore order and dispense justice, if there had been any hope that the king would act. But there was none. Henry VI seemed incapable of fulfilling the demands of his role. His inadequacy left a vacuum at the centre of the state. Though many must have wished to see it filled, only a minority wanted the king deposed: the last deposition of a king (Richard II) had happened within old men's lifetimes, and even if there had been a fine alternative candidate (which there was not), people knew that this was no sure and easy solution.

Failing the king, they had to look to the great lords, but few of these inspired confidence either. The best that could have been said of John Mowbray, third duke of Norfolk, was that he was better than most. He was a great man only in titles and possessions, not in personality, but he made some effort to do what was expected of a man in his position.

The little town of Framlingham in Suffolk had been the seat of the dukes of Norfolk for a good two centuries, ever since the huge loop of the castle had begun to take shape on the crown of the low hill above the town and the mere, the shallow lake that sat alongside it. Norfolk was the greatest of the non-royal dukedoms of England; its holder held by right of birth the position of earl marshal, one of the core offices of state. When the duke was in residence, not just the castle but the entire small town must have steamed with life. Men whom the duke needed to see, and men who needed to see the duke, would of necessity come there, and those who could not command lodgings in its castle would find them at the base of the hill. French as well as English could have been heard in the narrow streets, and Latin too, since there were plenty of priests attached to the duke's household and the church of St Michael in the town.

As well as the duke's own servants, there was space for independent businesses to grow to serve the household and its hangers-on. Some time in the early fifteenth century, members of the Calle family from Great and Little Waldingfield – small villages on the road from Sudbury to Lavenham, some miles to the south-west – came to Framlingham, and set up one such business, a grocer's shop.[1]

It was perhaps Simon Calle who started up the shop, but it is not clear whether he ever ran it. He probably made the money he needed to establish it from the farm he continued to run in the Waldingfields, and perhaps he intended from the start that the shop would be run mostly by his eldest son, John. Certainly John ran it later, probably from the mid-1440s. It seems to have been a thriving establishment. Grocers in this period were traders in dry goods: salt, sugar, dried fruits, spices and the like. (They would not have handled meat and fresh fish, vegetables, bread, or other foodstuffs that were readily available elsewhere.) Calle stocked local goods – candles made by a nearby chandler, the mustard that was grown in Norfolk – but he would also have stocked more exotic spices and other imported produce. The cosmopolitan men who visited and served the duke had demands greater than those that most village shopkeepers would have needed to meet, and John Calle would not only have bought stocks from merchants who came to Framlingham to sell to him, he and his staff would also have travelled – to Ipswich, to London, perhaps to other places too – to source the goods that their customers might require.

Richard Calle, the man at the centre of this story, was John's younger brother, probably the second of Simon Calle's five sons. (There was a daughter Margaret, too.) There was

Framlingham Castle

not the money to start businesses for all of them, so Richard grew up knowing that for as long as his brother lived, if he wished to be more than his assistant, or a farmhand in Great Waldingfield, he would have to tread another path.

The Calles were not great magnates, though they had land in both of the Waldingfields as well as the Framlingham shop. They were however an old and well-respected family, with reason to be proud of their heritage. Their family lore had it that they were descended from one of three Saxon brothers who had come to Britain in the eighth century. One had settled in Scotland, one in the West Country, and the one from which Richard's family stemmed in East Anglia. This was more legend than truth, most likely, but the same could have been said of the lineage of most noble families. The Calles had left a respectable trace in historical records for at least two hundred years before Richard's time. There had been clergy in the family, as well as smallholders and carpenters.

Simon and his wife Agnes got their sons educated, and Richard and his brothers profited well from their chances. There would not have been much opportunity for schooling in Great Waldingfield, so they were probably taught in Framlingham; indeed, it is possible that the family moved to the town largely so the boys could be schooled there. There were learned men in Framlingham, most of them connected to the church or the castle, and it was probably in a small school run by one such man that Richard and his brothers learned to read and write. As well as his native English, Richard picked up French well enough to

read books in the language, and Latin too. He was taught some accounting, and was able to keep business records.

Regnold, the third or fourth son, went into the church, but Richard did not take this course, and nor did Thomas and Robert, his other two brothers. Richard instead (and Thomas too) became an estate manager.[2] This was a role in which he would act as the representative of a landlord, managing their estates, collecting rents, paying expenses, passing messages to and fro, and dealing out justice on a small scale via the manor court. It was varied work, and a man who gained the trust of his employers could expect to take on a great deal of responsibility. He would travel around, meet a range of men and women, learn something of the wider world. If he would not quite grow rich, certainly he could become comfortable; he might earn enough to buy land of his own.

It is perhaps exaggerating to call this profession Richard's choice. His was not an era when men expected to choose their destiny. Many men did exactly what their fathers had done, though there were plenty of others for which this was not practicable, usually for reasons of money, or not desirable, for reasons of temperament and skill. These men mostly did whatever came their way as an alternative, and estate management was what came Richard's way. It was a suitable job for a young man with a bit of education, but not the family money or connections to do as the Paston sons had done and train as a lawyer, or the inclination to become a priest; for a man who had been brought up in the country and a small town, and who knew country ways.

At the outset of his career, he needed of course to find an employer. The Calles can have been in no doubt how he should set about this: they would ask the duke of Norfolk. As shopkeepers they were not, of course, intimates of the duke. But they were known to him, and this kind of service was part of what the duke was expected to do for his underlings. Indeed he did do so: Richard or his father, or both together, sent word to the duke that the boy needed a position, and word came back that he had been recommended to John Paston.[3]

The Calle family did what the dukes of Norfolk told them to do: always had, always would. So it was probably not a case of Richard considering whether the Pastons would suit him as employers, it was more that again, he accepted what was offered to him. He would not, most likely, have been indentured to the Pastons, or apprenticed to one of their more senior estate servants. He was not legally committed to working for the family for the rest of his life, or even for a fixed few years. But he must have taken it for granted that short of a major falling-out or an unexpected change in his or his employers' situations, he would be a servant of the Paston family from that time onwards.

And arguably working for the Pastons suited him pretty well. Serving a well-off gentry family was not the same as working for the duke himself, but perhaps this too was, if not quite a choice, at least a road down which he was happy to be guided. He seems to have been a strong-willed man, somewhat given to speaking his mind, and he maybe realized that the deference of being a nobleman's servant, the rigid protocol of a great household, would not come easily to him.

Gresham was a good way from Framlingham, and Richard a young lad; he perhaps knew nothing about the Pastons' troubles there before he accepted their offer of employment. And if he had known, it would most likely have made no difference. In an era when cathedral servants could be set upon, when farmers hid under their haybales and quaked, there were few safe jobs for any man. The Pastons were clearly a family whose estate management offered opportunities, and if it also might bring risks, well, that was the nature of life.

Norwich was near enough that he could come home to Framlingham sometimes – not frequently, but often enough to keep in touch with his family. He might find business with the duke, or call by on his way to London, where John Paston was known to spend much of his time. Paston village, Oxnead and most of the other family estates were farther away, but Margaret Paston's lands at Mautby were nearer. The circles of his old life and his new would overlap just a little: not too much, but perhaps that too was to Richard's advantage. In Framlingham men knew him as the grocer's son. In Norwich he had a chance to reinvent himself, and perhaps to grow to be something more.

Church of St Mary, Shelton, Norfolk

So on the whole he is likely to have been happy with the opportunity that had been offered him. Probably some time between 1449 and the early 1450s (we do not know exactly when) he packed his spare clothes, his quills and ink, his knife, and whatever else his family could spare for him, saddled his horse and set off for Norfolk and a new phase in his life.

The Calle family

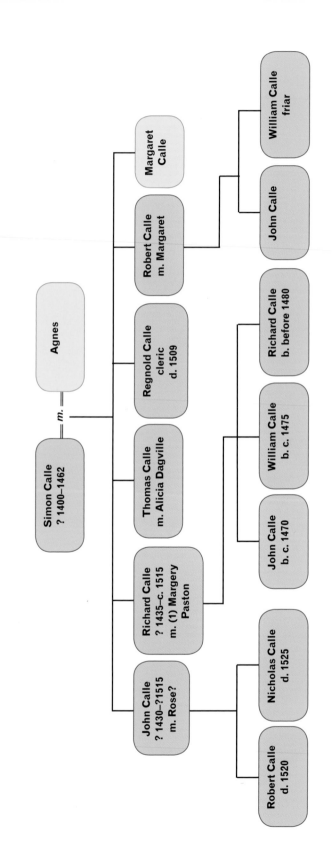

Note: information on the Calle family is limited, and this is a 'best guess' family tree.

Simon Calle
? 1400–1462

m.

Agnes

John Calle
? 1430–?1515
m. Rose?

Richard Calle
? 1435–c. 1515
m. (1) Margery Paston

Thomas Calle
m. Alicia Dagville

Regnold Calle
cleric
d. 1509

Robert Calle
m. Margaret

Margaret Calle

Robert Calle
d. 1520

Nicholas Calle
d. 1525

John Calle
b. c. 1470

William Calle
b. c. 1475

Richard Calle
b. before 1480

John Calle

William Calle
friar

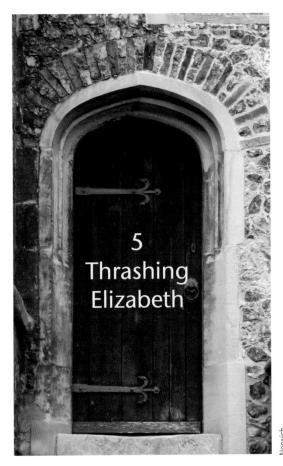

Norwich

M argery Paston was too young to remember the days just after her family left Gresham, when they lived in Grandma Paston's house, with beds and dishes borrowed from Grandma Paston's store.[1] By the time she was old enough to take notice, her parents had recovered their balance, replaced their wrecked and stolen household goods, and probably lived for most of the time in a good-sized house of their own in Norwich.

Norwich was a great city: not nearly as big as London, but one to rival any other city in England. It was large in size as well as population: a full square mile was enclosed by the recently built walls. There was open space within the walls, although most of it was private space, belonging to the castle, the cathedral, the churches and priories, the hospitals, and kept as gardens by the richest residents, men like the dukes of Norfolk and Suffolk. There were two big market places, one in Tombland by the cathedral, and one in the shadow of the church of St Peter Mancroft. There were perhaps sixty churches. And in the gaps between these great buildings and fenced-in spaces, and the shops and workshops that lined the main streets, the people of Norwich made their homes: the poor men and women living hugger-mugger in narrow alleys, the better-off like Margery's family in comfortable houses with a number of rooms.

The Pastons owned various houses in the city over the years. At one time they had a mansion called Paston House in what is now Crown Court off Elm Hill. They also owned

Princes Inn on Elm Hill itself. One of these two was probably Grandma Paston's home, though one Norwich historian[2] believed the family used Princes Inn 'as a sort of overflow house'.

Elm Hill – not very steep, though definitely on an incline – winds up from the open space of Tombland by the cathedral towards what was then the huge monastery of the Blackfriars. One side is close to the River Wensum, which makes a loop around the centre of Norwich. Princes Inn was on this side. It is not certain exactly where it stood, but it is possible that part of its fabric survives.

Such houses tended to be built with a main block set parallel to the road, and in some cases a second block set at right angles to it. The great hall was on the first floor, with other rooms below it, and typically a stone-vaulted cellar beneath them. In Norwich the upper floors were not built of stone, but of wood and brick, or perhaps wattle and daub, or the local flint. A path led through – via an archway, in the midst of or at the end of the block – to a back yard, surrounded by smaller buildings: the stables, the wood store, the buttery and kitchens. For a big estate like the ones Agnes and John Paston controlled, either in the side block or elsewhere leading off the yard there would be a room for their estate servants (men like Richard Calle, when they came to Norwich) to work in, and probably sleep in too. Beyond the yard and the stables, if there was space a garden was laid out; and for the houses that backed onto the river there was a landing stage, since many goods were transported by water.

At one time the Pastons also seem to have owned or rented a house in the parish of St Mary Coslany, an old round-towered church in the quieter northern area of the city. And a little later – perhaps around 1453 – they bought another house close to the church of St Peter Hungate, not far from Princes Inn.

Wherever Margery's home was situated, it would have been a busy household. The family themselves were of course at the centre of it, and Margery's mother Margaret must have seemed to her the centre of the family, since her father was so often away in London. Much of her focus was on managing the family's estates, and supervising the servants who did work connected with them: Margaret was no idle rich woman, and nor did she concentrate only on her growing family.

John II and John III, her elder brothers, would have been important

Church of St Peter, Ketteringham, Norfolk

Thought to be the sign from the Pastons' house (now in King Street, Norwich)

figures in the earliest
years of Margery's life, though later they were sent away to school and university and she
must have seen much less of them. Over the years there were to be three more brothers
who survived infancy, Edmund, Walter and William, and a sister, Anne. In addition there
were household servants: nursemaids for the children when they were small, cooks, housemaids, grooms and so on, as well as the estate servants and the other men of business who
acted for the family in connection with their wide-ranging affairs.

Father Gloys was a regular presence. He acted as spiritual guide and confessor to
both Margery's mother and her grandmother, and to the other family members. He was
among the people who wrote letters for Margaret and Agnes Paston, he collected rents
on occasion, and he probably also had a connection with one or more of the Norwich
churches.

Of course the household saw Grandma Paston and those children of hers who still lived
with her when Margery was young: Elizabeth, who was around twenty when Margery was
born, and when he was not away at school Clement, who was about eight years older than
Margery. Her uncle Edmund had died around the time she was born, in March1449.[3] He
was about twenty-four, and seems to have been healthy shortly before, so this was a sudden
and serious loss to the family, although as John Paston would have been well aware, it also
reduced to some extent the problem of sharing out their father's inheritance.

William, Margery's other uncle, had become a lawyer and spent most of his time in
London. He seems only rarely to have returned to Norwich. There was still a distance
between Margery's father and his brothers, and between him and his mother as well, but
Margaret Paston had not let John's quarrel become hers, and she seems to have worked to
stay on good terms with all of his family.

Once Margery grew past babyhood, she probably joined her mother in visiting with
the other good families of the county, and in entertaining them when they returned the
visits. Only on the biggest social occasions did the Pastons meet up with the nobility, but
there were plenty of gentry families: other lawyers, rich merchants, landowners. Although
there was no other girl close to her age in her own family (Anne was probably between
five and ten years younger), she must have met and spent time with the daughters of her
parents' friends and colleagues.

Norwich was a city known for its feuds and factionalism, and as well as friends, there

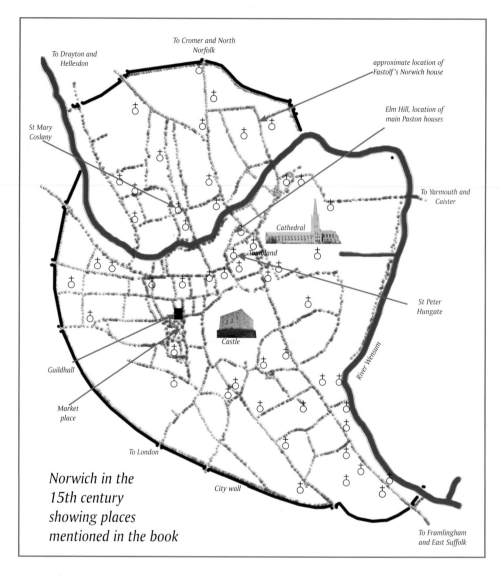

To Cromer and North Norfolk

To Drayton and Hellesdon

approximate location of Fastolf's Norwich house

Elm Hill, location of main Paston houses

St Mary Coslany

To Yarmouth and Caister

Cathedral

Tombland

St Peter Hungate

Castle

River Wensum

Guildhall

Market place

To London

Norwich in the 15th century showing places mentioned in the book

City wall

To Framlingham and East Suffolk

were those the Pastons called their enemies. But in a small city the factions were always loose, and marriages and links through work and public duties added to their complexity: even their worst enemies also had personal connections of sorts with the family.

Leather working and shoe making had been Norwich's trades for centuries, but at this time cloth working was coming to overtake them as a profession. The streets and alleys of Norwich were thick with buildings whose upper storeys had been built with wide arrays of windows to provide light for the weavers who worked in them. The city was thick with priests and friars too, and the acrid tang of tanning leather must have mingled with the sweet spicy scent of incense to make up the city's characteristic smell.

It was also a city that resounded with the clang of masons' chisels and tap-tap of carpenters' hammers, because it was a booming place that was showing its prosperity in fine buildings. The churches were mostly built of flint, since there was no good regular building stone in Norfolk: when the budget allowed, the pebbles were knapped into regular squares that shone like coal, or shaded water. St Mary's was getting a fine new nave and chancel, which sat oddly against its elderly tower, and most other churches in the city were being extended too. Over the years the Pastons contributed building funds to St Mary's, to St Peter Hungate, and perhaps to other churches as well. What they seem not to have done, though, was to establish the chantry chapel that Grandfather Paston had wanted, with priests who would sing masses for his soul. Margery's grandmother and her father had never managed to come to agreement on how this expensive arrangement would be paid for.

The family would have left Norwich when epidemics came to the city (as happened quite frequently) and the countryside was thought to be safer, and most likely in the summer, when their more rambling homes in the country did not need to be heated, and their servants (and John and Margaret too) could oversee the harvesting of their crops.

Each place they lived in was different. Paston, owned by Grandma Paston but probably used by all the family from time to time, with the hall set close by the church, and the flat expanse of the pebble beach and the wide North Sea only a few paces away; Oxnead – also Grandma's house – set amid water meadows and woodland, a comfortable house that had been extended by Grandfather and Grandma Paston, with a chapel and a grand hall; Mautby, in the marshy land inland from Yarmouth, Margery's mother's ancestral home. Grandma Paston had not remarried after her husband's death, and Grandmother Mautby had been widowed twice over, and was also now on her own. She probably stayed in her second husband's house, and in time Margaret Paston was to renovate Mautby Hall for her own use.

The Pastons probably did not go to Gresham often. The house that Margaret had lived in before the attack seems never to have been repaired, and the castle too had become little more than a ruin.

The rhythm of life would have been slower in the countryside, but the days probably passed in much the same activities in both places. There was a lot of prayer. Father Gloys could hold private services for them in the chapel at Oxnead, but in Norwich, and on the other estates where the Pastons had no chapel of their own, they would have taken their pew in the parish church. They also went sometimes to Bromholm Priory, a great religious centre close to Paston village which claimed to hold part of the True Cross of Christ; to Walsingham, the county's other great pilgrimage centre; to Norwich Cathedral and other famous churches in the region. They prayed for themselves, for the country, for their dead ancestors, for anything and everything the priests told them to pray for. They went to mass, to confession, listened to sermons. Death hovered at their shoulders always; the next world was almost as real to them as this one.

The high points of the year in Norwich were the great religious festivals, when processions through the city centre were arranged by the strong guilds that dominated the commerce of the city, and the two annual fairs. Margery must have been many times to the open ground outside the city for St Magdalen's fair in July and Carrow fair

Church of St Mary Magdalene, Mulbarton, Norfolk

in September, where she would have met with not just people she knew in Norwich, but men, women and children from across the county.

Although Margery's brothers were sent to school, and as they grew to university, this was not something that was generally done for girls. Margery knew, of course, what her future would be. She would marry. (The Pastons had no tradition of sending daughters to nunneries.) Then she would run a household, bear children, control servants, keep the household accounts, as far as she could. So she needed learning of a practical kind. She seems to have learned to read, and probably (though not certainly) to write. She would have picked up her letters from whoever was around to teach her: Father Gloys, the chaplains of friends' families who taught her with other girls, her mother and her grandmothers.

Almost all women spent much time in sewing and mending, and this would have been a sizeable part of Margery's routine as well.

In those days children were not indulged by modern standards. They were expected to make themselves useful, in whatever way suited their family's station. And they were disciplined harshly, since it was taken for granted that children, servants, and wives too needed to have obedience beaten into them. Margery was a girl in a family dominated by boys, which perhaps helped to give her an easier time than most. There is no indication that either her mother or her father were particularly brutal towards their children, but the same was not true of her Grandmother Paston.

Margery probably escaped more lightly than her aunt Elizabeth and uncle Clement,

but she must have known how they were treated, and it surely made her wary when she was with her grandmother. Grandmother Paston even took care to ensure that Clement was beaten regularly when he was away at school: 'if he has not done well,' she wrote in a note for herself and her servants, 'pray that his master will truly belash him till he will amend'.[4]

The worst of it was reserved for Elizabeth. At one stage (when Margery was eight or so) she was being thrashed once or twice a week, so severely that her mother drew blood.[5] Her head was battered, her skin broken and bruised, so she was unable to go out. The Pastons' friend and relative Elizabeth Clere even wrote to Margery's father to warn him how his sister was being treated and beg him to intervene, and probably talked to Margaret as well. (If any of them dared to speak to Agnes Paston, there is no indication that she took any notice.)

Elizabeth was heading into her late twenties, and not yet married: something unusual in these times. She was clearly a strong-willed, even headstrong woman who did not submit meekly to her mother's treatment. And she was desperate to leave home, but to do so she needed to be found a husband, or for arrangements to be made for her to board elsewhere, and neither had happened. She would not have been expected to find a husband for herself: with

Church of St Peter Hungate, Norwich

her father dead it was the responsibility of her eldest brother to negotiate a marriage for her, and the obligation of her mother to help and encourage him.

We can imagine the visits to Princes Inn: Margery crouching in the corner, perhaps with a doll to play with, while the ladies drank ale and ate cakes, and squabbled with each other like hissing cats. Some of their conversation was about suitors for Elizabeth: various men were mentioned from time to time, but they seem to have been a motley lot who did not prompt much enthusiasm from either Elizabeth or her family, and each time the negotiations dwindled away, or some more determined family stepped in and claimed the man for themselves.

Why had Elizabeth not been settled? There is nothing to tell us now, although the anger shown in those thrashings hints at a specific reason, and not just her brother and mother's failure to do what was necessary. Possibly there was a scandal: Elizabeth becoming entangled with an unsuitable man, or even the hushed-up birth of a baby. It might, though, have been no more than happenstance and bad fortune. She was the child of an elderly father, and perhaps Judge Paston had never quite fixed his thoughts firmly on getting her wed. Her mother had been an heiress, like Margaret Mautby, and had encountered no difficulty in finding a husband, so maybe she did not take it in that greater efforts would need to be made to settle her daughter. Then there was a time of confusion after the judge's death; there were the many demands on her eldest brother's resources, the chaos at Gresham, the worries about the friar who claimed Oxnead … somehow the years passed, and getting Elizabeth married off never quite reached the centre of her family's attention.

Elizabeth had most likely sunk into depression, because her mother's tart comments later suggest that she was not notable for making herself useful. She had at last been found, not a husband but at least a place, in the household of Lady Pole. Her mother's note on this was, 'say to Elizabeth Paston that she must use herself to work readily, as other gentlewomen do, and somewhat to help herself therewith'.[6]

Perhaps Margery knew what had gone wrong with Elizabeth's life, but perhaps she did not, and took the situation for granted. That her grandmother was barbed and edgy, that her mother had more of the easy temperament of the Mautbys and Berneys, that Uncle William never came home: this was simply how life was. She surely realized, though, that it was not a happy situation for a woman to fail to marry; she surely hoped not to find herself in Elizabeth's position.

After Elizabeth left for Lady Pole's establishment she never returned home permanently, and Margery probably saw her only a handful of times during the remainder of their lives.

Church of St Peter Hungate, Norwich

The Paston family

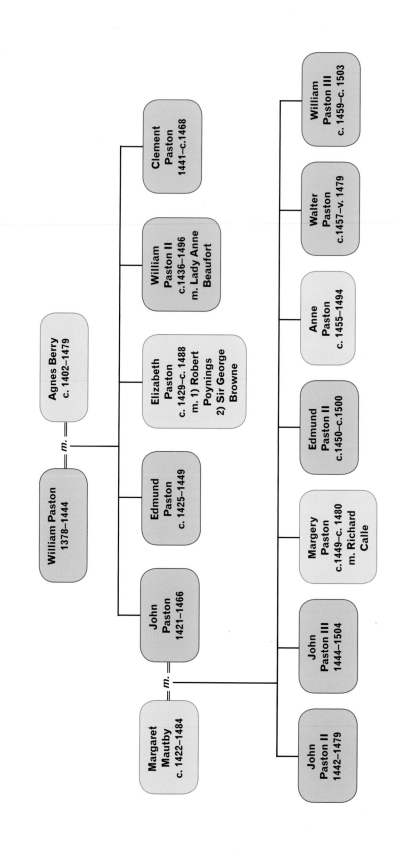

6
The wheat, the malt

Bromholm Priory, Norfolk

As a young lad, Richard Calle would probably not have hired lodgings of his own. His job called for him to travel a great deal, and he would have spent its early months getting to know the pattern of the Paston estates. They must have owned a house on many, if not all, of them where the family and their servants stayed when they travelled to check on their tenants and collect their dues, and Richard and his colleagues would have opened these houses up, lit fires, hunkered down side by side in the chamber each night. The roads were dangerous, and so was some of their work – which at times required them to carry sizeable sums of money – so they would have kept in groups of two, three or more, not travelled alone. And Richard was an educated man, worth a good salary; he would have left the dogsbody work of tending fires, cooking supper and grooming the horses to lower servants.

The men would have carried their bedding with them in their saddlebags, and Richard must have mixed his ink and sharpened his quills in dusty counting houses and parlours in houses that had sometimes not been lived in for months. In Norwich he would have slept with the other servants in the quarters set aside for them; and where no Paston house was available he probably stayed at a roadside inn.

He talked with the other servants who worked on the estate affairs, watched them, and learned from them the practicalities of his job, to add to the booklearning he had acquired in Framlingham. He knew how to write and to reckon accounts: now he needed to know how to go about judging the quality of potential tenants, agreeing terms for letting land, getting in rents, selling crops from the land that the family farmed direct, running the manor courts, and so on. Men like John Damme and John Bacton, and the other gentlemen of Norfolk who worked with and for the Pastons, would have been good guides to all this practical knowledge. There is no sense in the letters that survive that Richard became close to Father Gloys, but he had to work with the man, and seems to have done so successfully, so perhaps he learned from him too.

He also talked with the tenant farmers, and the merchants who bought the meat and wool from the sheep, the wheat and barley, and got some sense of how they saw his employers. And of course, he took instructions from his master and mistress.

If there was a clear social divide between a family and their household servants (their cooks, grooms, housemaids, laundrymaids and so on), there was less of one between a landowner and his men of business. John Paston used a wide variety of men to help handle his and Margaret's estates, and some of them at least – like Damme and Bacton – were landowners in their own right, with servants of their own. If there was a form of graduation, with the Pastons employing those less affluent than themselves, and John Paston doing most of his legal work for those who were richer than him, still it was no more than rough. But the Pastons, like many people of their times, were very status-conscious, and they saw themselves as having a higher rank in society than Richard and his family. John was a lawyer who worked for pay, and did not live only on the income from his estates, but his legally oriented work was considered more prestigious than the kind of administrative work that Richard did for him. And although rich merchants were among the most powerful men in Norwich, keeping shops like the one the Calles ran in Framlingham was also seen by the Pastons as something done by those below them in social position.

Richard worked primarily for the Pastons, and was closely tied to them, but he probably also did work on occasion for other people. The ability to write was useful to many who lacked it, so particularly when Richard came to one of the Pastons' smaller or more remote estates, the places where the family rarely ventured, Father Gloys was not often seen and the resident priest had little learning, he was most likely called on to write out formal agreements, or set down on paper any letters that needed to be sent. Many people did not travel much if at all, and Richard would also have been used to take messages with him when he returned to Norwich, or to bring the farmers and their families goods that were needed from the city. The payment for these small services would not have been large, but it enabled him to save, and to plan to buy land of his own in time.

Later in his career Richard travelled to London, certainly on several occasions and perhaps regularly, to liaise with John Paston and the other members of the family who made their lives there, to carry letters and to do business. But in the first years of his career he was probably in Norfolk much, if not all, of the time. He maybe left the county only on the occasions (probably regular, but not frequent) when he went to see his family across the Suffolk border in Framlingham.

What survives today of Richard are some of the letters he wrote to the Pastons, and others he wrote for them: he was a competent scribe, and several members of the family dictated their letters to him. His words are generally formal, and cautiously phrased; his own opinions emerge only occasionally, and sideways. So it is difficult to judge now what were his private thoughts about his employers. The best we can do

Edingthorpe, near Paston, north Norfolk

is to see for ourselves what comes across of them from their letters, and guess at what he might have made of it.

They probably struck him as a fractious family. In their own way they were a close one, but they argued frequently and bitterly. Richard could hardly have failed to notice that although Margaret acted to some extent as a go-between, there was a gulf between Agnes Paston and her eldest son. The two senior Pastons had separate households, and ran separate groups of estates, largely independently of each other. Richard must have had some dealings with Agnes, but as far as we can judge he was John and Margaret's servant, and did not generally act for her. (He might however have been based at her Norwich house, if that was the place where the Pastons had suitable accommodation for their men of business.) Agnes's surviving letters focus on her business affairs and her problems: they rarely deal with happy events, so it is little wonder that she comes across in them as bitter and crabbed. Perhaps in life she was more capable of laughter and joy than her letters suggest, but she was not of Richard's generation, and there is no reason to think he ever became close to her.

Agnes was rich, very rich. Indeed by Richard's standards – by any standards but those of the great nobles – all the Pastons were very rich. Richard would have been aware, since it was widely known across East Anglia, that their fortunes had been built up almost entirely by the judge, through his business and later his marriage. This gave them something of the shiny impermanence of gilt jewellery. It was probably assumed by many people that the judge had made his fortune not just through his intellectual brilliance, but through ruthlessness, and perhaps at times bending the rules. He had never been caught taking bribes, but he was certainly suspected of having gained unfair advantage from the estates of elderly widows he acted for.[1]

In 1451 a taxation list was drawn up for Norwich, which John and Agnes Paston clearly regarded as their main home, since both featured on the list of taxpayers.[2] Some of the Norfolk gentry would not have declared their income in Norwich, but a number of big names did. The annual income John Paston declared – £66 – was the joint second highest amount in the city. Agnes, declaring an annual income of £40, was also comfortably in the top twenty for this, probably the second largest (and second richest) city in England. Neither the Pastons nor the other rich merchants and gentry of Norwich would have been totally honest with the taxman (there is evidence that John took soundings to find out what other men were admitting to before declaring his own income), but this is likely to reflect their relative affluence fairly well.

These were not rich people who were free with their money, though. On the contrary, almost all the Pastons were to complain regularly, throughout the period when Richard worked for them, about their shortage of cash. Agnes had no reason to grumble, but she did not spend her money to help her children, or to establish her husband's memorial: she evidently saw those as John's responsibilities. Margaret complained to John about her lack of good clothes and jewels; John's brothers, William and Clement, complained that they had not been allocated enough of their father's estate; Elizabeth suffered from a shortage of dowry sufficient to attract the kind of husband her family wanted for her; a generation on, John's sons would complain too of a chronic shortage of ready cash. At times the family's servants were not paid their wages promptly, and there must have been grumbles in the servants' halls as well.

Were they actually property rich but cash poor? It is hard to say. Perhaps John did have money problems, since he was trying to maintain a lifestyle on the scale of his father's with far fewer lands to support it. The costs of defending Gresham, the money and possessions lost when it was taken from them, the costs of claiming it back, would all have taken their toll. (However, later in life he was to claim that in this period he had had no difficulty in putting away a good sum in savings each year.[3]) But Richard could perhaps have been forgiven if he had judged not only John, but all the Pastons, to be not just seriously rich, but seriously mean.

With Margaret, Richard seems to have been on respectful but good terms. Like her husband she was older than him, but only by ten years or so, not the full generation that separated him from Agnes. There was much to admire in her: not just her bravery at Gresham, but her competence and energy in running the Norfolk end of the family affairs. She consulted with her husband (as Richard knew, since he sometimes wrote out the letters in which she did so), but took decisions for herself as well. He might have had little to do with Margaret's own inherited estates in his first years with the family: Margaret was needed on the Paston lands, and seems to have spent little time at Mautby. But he would have taken in Margaret's high opinion of her own family, which was indeed an older-established and in many ways better respected one than the Pastons, and her fondness for them too. As well as the uncle who had so singularly failed to help her at Gresham, Margaret had a wide tranche of relations in south Norfolk, including a connection of sorts to Sir John Fastolf, a major figure in the county.

There was rather less to admire in John, but perhaps as a young man, conventionally deferential to his seniors, it took Richard some time to notice that; and even then he maybe did not pass a harsh judgement to himself, let alone to others. John seems to have been a diligent, if less than inspired, lawyer. He had the respect of major clients. He was less diligent over some of his family responsibilities, as the still unmarried sister, the still unbuilt chantry for his father, made all too apparent. But a generous man's verdict might have been that he was a man with more demands on his time and his resources than he was able to fulfil, and that it was understandable enough that he should let the sun rise and set each day without doing much about many of them.

Although John Paston seems not to have been a natural bully, or a man who relished confrontation, he had a tendency to get into trouble. True, many men saw violence in the early 1450s; the attack on John that took place by the cathedral door was not an isolated incident. But many men did not, and John Paston was never one of them. He was accused several times in his life of riotous behaviour, and his relations with Judge Yelverton, a formidable colleague of his father's, became difficult after 1456, when a servant of Yelverton's, one Wormegey, was killed in a fight. It is not clear exactly what happened, and Paston was not found guilty of the man's murder (while other men were), but Yelverton clearly attached some blame to him for the incident.[4]

Paston worked with a range of other men, as his position demanded, and had plenty of acquaintances, but seems not to have had a gift for friendship. As far as we can judge from what survives of him, he was no natural master either, and took minimal personal interest in his servants. He found it hard to delegate, hard to trust others. He took a close, even obsessive, interest in every aspect of the family's affairs, and when he was away from Norfolk he sent detailed instructions to his wife and his servants, in letters and doubtless

Church of St John the Baptist, Mileham, Norfolk

in spoken messages too. He had been brought up in the law, but even for a lawyer he was notably litigious on his own behalf; his life was a long procession of lawsuits against others, petitions to the king and his counsellors, battles to obtain what he believed was his due.

Perhaps John's saving grace was his wife, who seems always to have been loyal and supportive, even if she was greatly tried by her husband at times, and seems too to have been less naturally abrasive than her husband. He was also fortunate in the loyalty of most of his servants, Richard included. Richard evidently had much more of a knack for getting on with others, and in this way he complemented his master just as Margaret did.

One of the early letters that Richard wrote to John Paston (estimates of its date vary, from 1450 to 1460) gives a sense of the work he was doing for the Pastons at this time. He must still have been a young man, but clearly he was being entrusted with a wide variety of by no means easy tasks. He wrote from Hainford, a short way north of Norwich, perhaps when he was en route back to the city from Gresham. (Hainford was not Paston land, it belonged to Sir John Fastolf, so Richard either stayed there because it was convenient, or was carrying out errands for the Fastolf estate.) The letter was addressed to John in (as he often was) 'London at the Inner Temple'.[5]

Much of the letter was about Gresham. After the disastrous events of the late 1440s, it was a major task for the Pastons' estate servants to ensure that the farms were occupied again, the fields restored to good order, and the estate to profitability. James Rockerson, the man James Gloys and the other men at Gresham had distrained a few years earlier, was not mentioned again, so perhaps he was among those who left the estate when Partridge and his men were terrorizing its inhabitants.

Richard suggested that John start a legal action against one James Gatte, who had opposed his attempts to take control, and that his own name should

Church of St Mary Magdalene, Mulbarton, Norfolk

be attached to it. He had persuaded several of the old tenants to return to the lands they had abandoned, and 'found a means that all your lands shall be let as well as ever they were'. In this he had enlisted the help of Robert Coole, a tricky business because John Paston was involved in a legal action against the man: which he should drop, please, Richard asked, because 'he is the most able man to take a farm of land that I know in your lordship'.

He also asked John to take action against a man called Robert Wight, or sometimes Furbisher. The Pastons' man at Matlask, another of their estates in north Norfolk, had seized the cattle of a tenant called Lightfoot when he had not paid his dues, and while they were held on the Pastons' bond ground this Wight had broken down the garden dyke and carried off a two-year-old bullock.

Finally, he passed on the local news and gossip. My lord of Worcester (the bishop, whom the Pastons regarded as an important patron) was at Blakeney; and John Wymondham, one of the Pastons' enemies, had entered an estate he claimed at Felbrigg, only to be 'put out' by the commons.

All this was lively and confident, but he wrote with formality, as men did in his times. His letter was addressed to his 'right reverent and most worshipful Master', and he signed it 'your poor servant and bedeman, Ric. Calle'. A bedeman, or beadsman, was one who prayed for another (the name derives from the rosary beads that people counted while saying their prayers): not a cleric (Richard was never one of those), but a subordinate, as Richard knew himself to be.

Although he seems to have grown into his job quite quickly, and by the mid-1450s was firmly established as one of the Pastons' senior servants, there are hints of friction too. That is hardly surprising for a man in his position, working to gain profit from estates in troubled and dangerous times. Whatever rents he gathered, whatever action he took against men in arrears, whatever price he managed to negotiate for their malt (much of their arable land was put to barley, so this was a major crop for them), it would not be quite as much as his masters had hoped, or so it must often have seemed. Both John and Margaret were clearly demanding people to work for, and John was not always an appreciative one.

There is a hint of past disagreements, for instance, in a letter Richard wrote to John probably in 1455.[6] He will not distrain the tenants' goods again till he hears from John, he writes. Indeed, he and his colleagues will do nothing in future without asking first for his master's advice. There must have been some earlier disagreement to make him write in this vein, and he had obviously been given a very firm message afterwards. You work for us; you obey our orders; you do only what we have told you to do.

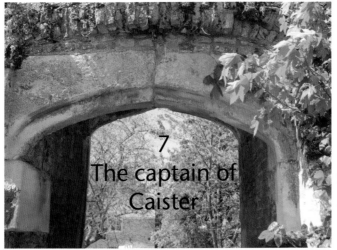

7
The captain of Caister

Sir John Fastolf is not easy for us to pigeonhole today, and quite likely he flummoxed his contemporaries to some extent too. He was a soldier, a captain in the later stages of the Hundred Years War, and a very successful one. His servant William Worcester listed his positions: king's counsellor; grand master of the household of John, regent of the Kingdom of France and duke of Bedford; governor of Anjou and Maine; captain of Mantes, Alencon, Fresnay-le-Vicomte, the Bastille in Paris, Honfleur, Harfleur, Port Meulan, the palace of Rouen ('he made the very strong tower there above the river Seine on the east side'), Fecamp, Caen (he 'made the counterwall on the south-east side of the Castle towards the gate'), lieutenant captain of the castle of Calais, Sieur Bekecrespyn, Sieur Dourechyr, captain and baron of Sillé le Guillaume, marshal of Normandy, grand butler of Normandy, and constable of Bordeaux.[1]

But with all this renown, Fastolf never did as his great contemporaries did, and rose into the aristocracy. Possibly that was his own choice, either conscious or subconscious. Perhaps he was simply too abrasive, too unpopular with the men at court to receive that honour, particularly when he took in his old age to sending the king's council lengthy letters full of unsolicited advice.

He was also very rich, and most of the money came from his soldiering. He was not alone in having made a profit out of the war, but few, if any, others did quite as splendidly as Sir John. He amassed profits from every post, every action, and unlike other captains he was never taken prisoner, and forced to pay out a chunk of them in ransom. Perhaps as a result, men did not look kindly on him when he took a misstep: indeed at Patay in 1429, when his fellow commanders were all captured and he alone skipped free, there were rumours of cowardice, though Sir John would doubtless have argued that sheer prudence prevented him from following the others into a French dungeon.

And he spent his money. He maintained a large household, though an eccentric one: it majored in men of letters and retired men of war, and a few men – like Christopher Hanson, who ran his London affairs – who fitted both of these categories. William Worcester, the one-eyed Welshman who drew up that list of his appointments, rates as one of the first real English antiquaries. Fastolf had a large house in Southwark, on the south bank of the Thames, and another big house in Norwich. He owned such a huge chunk of Norfolk and Suffolk that eight thousand sheep grazed on his meadows. He had his own fleet of ships to handle his wool exports. This was not the Pastons' kind of affluence, it was a sizeable climb above them.

Finally, Fastolf spent a large wedge of his money in building a castle. This was – and still is – at Caister, a few miles from Yarmouth and barely a mile and a half from Margaret Paston's old family home at Mautby. It was a very grand castle, built in brick, in the style of the castle at Falaise that Sir John knew from his time in France, set around two large rectangular courtyards, with warrens of rooms – more than fifty in all – and a great hall that Worcester measured to be '38 of my paces long, which make 59 feet, and 16 paces or 28 feet wide'. It cost him more than £6,000, and took many years to complete.

The irony was that he did so when he was already an old man, and could not expect to spend more than a few years living in his castle when it was finished. He moved there permanently in 1454, when he was 74 years old. Nor did he do all this for his heir, because he had no obvious heir. His wife (by then long dead) had been some years older than him, and although she had had a son by an earlier marriage, she and Fastolf had had no children together. There were other relatives – a couple of nephews – but these drifted in and out of favour, and no one was clearly lined up to claim Caister and all Sir John's other estates when the old soldier headed to his Valhalla.

Margaret Paston was related to Sir John, though not closely. This provided a connection for the Pastons to build on, and both John and Margaret made good use of it. John began to work regularly for Fastolf when the old knight was still based in Southwark, and by the time the move to Caister came, he was among his most trusted advisers. He travelled regularly to Caister, and to Yorkshire, where Fastolf also had sizeable land holdings. This lucrative connection was one of several elements that ensured that as the 1450s wore on, life for the Pastons became more secure and comfortable. These were not easy times for the country at large, where Henry VI's continuing problems (he became insane for a while around 1453), and the increasing influence of the duke of York, meant matters were sliding steadily towards major conflict. But for the Pastons and their servants, they were good years.

The coastline of Norfolk has changed greatly over the centuries, and it is not easy to reconstruct how it appeared five hundred and fifty years ago. The far east of the county is very flat. The walled coastal town of Yarmouth stands on a relatively dry stretch of gravelly land, but scarcely a hill, and behind it pools the vast expanse of Breydon Water, and an even larger spread of marshes – Halvergate, Wickhampton, Runham and Mautby, and more – that are cut through by the rivers Bure, Yare and Waveney. Today much of this has been reclaimed, but in the Pastons' day it was partly open estuary and partly wet marsh, useful for growing reeds for thatching, for fishing and for hunting wildfowl, but much of it not fit for growing crops or even for grazing sheep.

Mautby and Caister are both north of Yarmouth, and today are some distance inland, but in those days they were intimately linked to the sea. Both places sat on what were effectively islands in the marshland. Channels of water, some nearer to ditches than canals, connected them with each other and with the Bure (running just south of them) as well as other rivers and channels to the north. The Bure curves northwards farther inland, and there was a navigable channel running most if not all of the way to Paston village; the Yare runs west, and is still navigable as far as Norwich. Roman ruins punctuate this area: there

Caister Castle

are the remains of forts at Caister itself, south of Breydon Water at Burgh, and close to Norwich at another place called Caistor.

Just as at Gresham, Mautby church was set on a high point of the dry land, and the hall was a half-mile away, down by the marsh and the fishponds. It had probably not been lived in since Margaret's mother remarried and moved away, but in these years Margaret seems to have begun to restore it for the family's use. Both Fastolf and the Pastons made some efforts to dredge the canal that linked Mautby with Caister, the Pickerill Fleet, and building materials could be brought to Caister's barge house from the open sea, and from there to Mautby via the canal. There were perhaps too many trees on the drier land for the Great Tower of Caister Castle (a hundred feet tall) to be visible from Mautby Hall itself, but it would have stood out prominently to anyone who made the short journey between the two, by barge, horse or foot.

Even in an era where much travel was done by water, these must have seemed remote places; and they were distant, not least, from the unrest that was so evident in Norwich and London. The community that built up around the hall and castle – Fastolf's household servants, his lawyers and other men of business, the Paston family and its servants, the farmers, builders, fishermen who worked for and with both households – was tightly self-contained. It was not isolated, though: Fastolf's tentacles stretched a long way.

Richard Calle was not quite of this community. His work for the Pastons was focused elsewhere, and his only reason for coming to Caister was to meet up with John and Margaret Paston when they were there, as they seem to have been increasingly often during the later 1450s. So his visits were perhaps not frequent, but they were regular enough that he would have come to know Worcester, Fastolf's secretary Thomas Howes, and the rest of his men of business. Here and elsewhere in Norfolk he must have met the other lawyers – men like Judge Yelverton – who also acted for Fastolf, and were jostling politely, but determinedly, for position in his hierarchy of advisers. He also went to the Southwark house during his journeys to London, and met Christopher Hanson and his team.

Many of Fastolf's servants were close to their master's generation. William Worcester was younger than most, perhaps in his forties in these years, and had married late, so he had a young family. But he was the kind of man who seems old before his time. Richard might not have become close friends with these men, but in his chats with them when he had to wait for his master, or to stay overnight at the castle, he would have learned something of the issues that concerned him.

It would have been evident to them all not only that John Paston put great store on his relationship with the elderly knight, but that Sir John was genuinely fond of his young lawyer. John Paston was nothing like Fastolf's troop of old soldier-retainers. When he was offered a knighthood around 1457, he chose to pay a fine rather than to accept the honour and the military obligations that came with it. Arguably that risked annoying old Fastolf, but this was one relationship that Paston seemed to fathom well, and Sir John did not hold it against him.

Fastolf might have been a profitable client, but he was not an easy one. He was descending into a spectacularly grouchy old age. He played his lawyers off blatantly against each other, and he piled on them mostly petty, tedious work: worries that his agents were not dealing fairly with his estates, negotiations over loans and debts, even nagging fears that men were being rude about him behind his back.[2]

Church of St Peter and St Paul, Bardwell, Suffolk

John Paston was none too bad at this kind of work, however. Showy arguments in the lawcourts do not seem to have been his forte: keeping papers in order, chasing small queries, offering flattery and reassurance, was stuff that must have suited him much better.

So how exactly did Paston reckon to profit out of all this dancing attendance on the old knight? Because it must have been clear to Richard, and to Fastolf's servants too, that he did hope to profit from it, and not just in reluctantly paid fees for services rendered. John was showing the same close cunning that he had employed when his father died: he evidently had a plan. It would have helped the two men's servants if they knew what it was, but even if Richard ruminated over the possibilities with Worcester and Howes, he was most likely left none too sure of the answer.

Fastolf was not the type to be generous in his lifetime, so it would come down to what he put in his will. Was there any chance he would make John Paston his heir? It probably seemed unlikely to Richard and the others. The connection was too distant, the nephews too present. Paston's best bet was to improve the links between the two families by engineering a marriage. Fastolf's closest living relatives were all men, so he would need to use one of the women in his own family to achieve this. Since Sir John had no apparent enthusiasm for either his nephews or his stepson, an attractive and ingratiating wife to any one of them might sway his choice of heir.

Elizabeth Paston needed a husband. She was too old for the nephews, but at a pinch she might have made a match with Fastolf's stepson Stephen Scrope. It was not one most women would have welcomed, since Scrope was a widower many years her senior, who admitted himself that he was physically repulsive. But John Paston pursued the possibility for a while, and Elizabeth was desperate enough that she expressed herself willing to consider the man.[3] It had come to nothing, though, by the time Elizabeth was packed off to Lady Pole's. Then in 1458 the Pastons' associates heard that a marriage had at last been

agreed for her. Her new husband, a Kentish man called Robert Poynings, had some connections with Fastolf and his servants, but he was never apparently seen as a candidate to inherit the estates.

Paston's daughters were small children still. They would not have been married at such an age, but a betrothal could have been agreed. It was probably known in the household that John Paston was casting around for a good match for Margery, and indeed that other families were making approaches about her to him. The nephews were mentioned, but the idea seems never to have gone beyond the kind of vague suggestion that Elizabeth had starved on a diet of for over a decade.

Church of St Peter and St Paul, Bardwell, Suffolk

Then Fastolf spelled out his own intentions, and it looked as if whatever scheming John Paston had done would all go to waste. Sir John had decided to found a college of monks at Caister, and to commit a large chunk of the income from his estates to funding it.[4]

This was a plan much like the one Judge Paston had formulated (and his son and widow had still not fulfilled), though on a rather larger scale. It had a charitable element to it (a group of poor men were to be supported as well as the monks), but in essence it was selfish. It was generally believed that after death, the souls of those neither so virtuous as to head straight for heaven, nor so villainous as to be condemned for good to hell, would spend a period in purgatory. This would be nasty and painful, but the souls in purgatory might hope through their agonies to atone for their sins, and eventually make a delayed ascent to eternal bliss. Meanwhile the atonement could be speeded through prayer on

behalf of the individual. So Sir John was planning to invest his cash in the comfort of his immortal soul.

There was not much joy for most of his servants in that decision. They could only hope that enough would be left, by the time the college had been funded and the nephews had been provided for, to create the legacies that they had all been promised. Worcester, Hanson, Howes and the rest had worked for the irascible old knight for years. They depended on him to leave them a little house perhaps, and a small annuity, not just because it was customary for a man in his position, but because they would face a cold and hungry old age if he did not do so.

For the lawyers, it was less bad news. A foundation such as this required a licence from the crown, and it also required a fee to be paid. This was not perverse, but part of a deliberate policy to discourage such foundations. There was irony in the fact that dozens of priests said prayers for the dead, when many parishes had no priest with any learning to tend to their living souls.

Fastolf had plenty of money, but no willingness to pay the kind of sums that were being mentioned. His lawyers would need to negotiate to try to get them lowered. They could probably spin that out for years, and while they were doing it, work on the old knight to change his mind.

St Mary's Church, Shelton, Norfolk

8
A
mention
in the
will

Lavenham, Suffolk

S ome people go through life like a cat. They look to find a secure niche where they can curl up, and do no more thereafter than is needed to get the necessities. Others hurl themselves at life, terrier-wise, impatient, seeking excitement, noticing the dangers only too late.

What little we know of Richard Calle suggests he was neither of these types. He was not lazy, and nor was he impetuous. The concept of a career was alien to most men of his era, but they were not unfamiliar with the concepts of bettering oneself and getting on, and it seems as if Richard took care to plan his life in the hope of doing just those things.

An estate manager's life, working for a family who owned a moderate spread of land, was not one that offered dramatic opportunities, but there were ways in which he could expand his role, and apparently Richard did so. At some point he moved out of the servants' hall and took a house of his own.[1] It would have been in Norwich, since that was the fulcrum around which his life turned, but since few traces survive of his life in these years we do not know where in the city it was.

He would have needed a servant or two, though he would not have set up the kind of large establishment that the Pastons ran. He probably opted for no more than one man, or perhaps a boy: to light the fire, sweep the yard, groom his horse; to mind the place when he was travelling and take messages for him. He did not need a cook. There were taverns in Norwich, and meals to be had in the Pastons' hall.

He could have taken a wife at this point, but he did not. It seems likely that he planned here too. He was not the heir to a great fortune, and no one would push him into a marriage for the family's sake; nor was he a serf who would settle for whatever company he could get. He must have wanted a wife with something of his own characteristics: a level-headed, careful woman, with a bit of learning and the willingness to acquire some more; with the ability to keep books, run a house, and help him with his enterprises.

Margaret Paston was a pretty good template. He could have done with a competent, intelligent, unflustered, hard-working wife like her. But there was no rush: he could afford to wait till he found the right woman. And the longer he waited, the better position he would be in to win the kind of woman he wanted.

The Pastons' estate staff do not seem to have had a clear hierarchy. Everyone reported to Margaret and John. But as Richard became more senior, he probably hired a lad or two who could work not only for him, but through him for his masters. That way he could take on more work, do the more demanding parts of it himself, and pass on to others the routine chores. That way he could continue to put money aside, and perhaps in time buy an estate of his own.

Rent collectors cannot hope to be universally popular, and many of them are quite the opposite. Force and terror are one way of driving tenants to pay their dues, but there are other ways too. There is no sign that Richard was a man given to bullying and violence, and some indication that he was a man who made friends widely and readily. In such a job it was in his interests to be on good terms with a broad range of men. As well as the Pastons' current tenants, there were men who might in time become their tenants; as well as the merchants they dealt with, there were those who might offer better terms in future. And these were troubled times, so even when things were going smoothly, it was useful for a man to do good deeds for others and to know that he might call on them in turn for help, if and when he needed it. It was useful too to learn to smell trouble in the air, and to make plans to take shelter when strong winds began to blow.

Neither John nor Margaret Paston seem to have confided unnecessarily in Richard, but as the years passed and he became more trusted he wrote more letters for Margaret, and sometimes for John as well, and was often charged with carrying verbal messages too between the two of them, and between them and their other servants. He learned not only what the Pastons wanted him to know, but doubtless quite a lot that they wished he did not have to know. By the time Sir John Fastolf took to his bed and prepared to die, he must have gained a good idea of how John Paston's plans in that direction had evolved.

The college of monks had not yet been authorized, and it would not now be founded in Fastolf's lifetime. The old knight no longer had the drive and energy to do it, and his grudges, his changes of mind, his anger at the fees demanded, meant that by this time his lawyers did not have to work to delay the project; it delayed itself. But Sir John was determined that the college should be established, so he would need to appoint someone to found it after his death. John Paston was working to ensure that this someone would be him.

In the last months of his life Fastolf was continually having new wills drafted, and John

Paston was the man who was drafting them for him. John Paston's legal work was not the subject of Richard's own work, but he probably knew this, because it was of such pressing interest to many of those he dealt with regularly. William Worcester, for instance, apparently never considered working for another master after Fastolf died.[2] In his own way, he was focused as intensely on John Paston on getting what he wanted out of Fastolf's will.

Worcester and his colleagues must have asked John Paston, as often as they dared, if their legacies were specified in the drafts. They probably got at best a vague and dismissive answer. Paston was the son of a rich man, and had always been comfortable, never known hunger. He did not instinctively understand the worries of those in less easy circumstances. And he was quite different in temperament from Richard: it did not come as naturally to him to chat with the servants and involve himself in their concerns. So it might have been simply than he was failing to provide reassurance, but it probably seemed more likely to Fastolf's servants that he was failing to remind Sir John of their needs.

One thing might have given them some reassurance. They probably had a good sense that although plenty of drafts of wills had been produced, Fastolf had not actually signed and had witnessed any of them.

As Fastolf's death approached, the atmosphere at Caister must have become more difficult; dense in a way apparent even to occasional visitors like Richard. Doctors and priests circled the deathbed. Worcester was nagging and worrying. Fastolf was still consulting a wide variety of lawyers, and talking of appointing close on a dozen executors. John Paston was talking to some of Fastolf's servants – Thomas Howes, for instance, seemed to be in favour – and not to others like Worcester. This made for irritability and suspicion.

Caister Castle

More surprisingly, John Paston was talking to his brothers. Richard probably knew this from his trips to London. He had had some dealings over the years with William Paston, who was well established as a lawyer now, and must have met occasionally too with Clement, who was preparing to join William and John at the Inns of Court.

Everyone close to the family would have heard something of what had happened when old Judge Paston died, of his eldest son's wily determination, and his action so speedy it crossed the border into disrespect for the dead. They knew of the feud that had resulted. But it was apparent it was being buried now, and it was not difficult to guess why. John Paston had a new plan, and he needed help to carry it off. It must have looked as if he was going to act in much the same way again, except that instead of acting against his brothers, this time he would act with them, and against most, if not all, of the other men who might claim to inherit or control Fastolf's estate.

That was not something that Richard, if he guessed at it, would have chosen to share with Fastolf's servants.

So except for Howes, and perhaps one or two others who had been taken into John Paston's confidence in advance, they were taken by surprise – as were Judge Yelverton and the other men who had been talked of as executors – when as soon as Fastolf stopped breathing, the Pastons snapped into action. They took steps to secure a range of Fastolf's goods across the whole span of his properties.[3] His money disappeared into 'safe keeping'. And when this was done, John Paston produced a will.

The watchers had not missed a signing session. Paston did not pretend that there had been one. This was an unsigned will. But that was irrelevant, he claimed: he had witnesses who would confirm that it reflected Fastolf's stated intentions. It agreed that he would pay into the estate a relatively modest sum, which would enable the college of priests to be licensed and founded. In return, he would receive all of Fastolf's lands and possessions.

Church of St Mary,
Saxlingham Nethergate, Norfolk

9
The
tapestries,
the silver,
the wine

Norwich

History does not record whether young Margery Paston ever met Sir John Fastolf. If she did so, it would have been briefly, in the way that pretty young girls are introduced to powerful aged men: curtsey when you come into the room; whatever you do, do not wrinkle your nose at the smell; smile, and agree with whatever he says to you; sing a song perhaps, or recite a poem, if anyone suggests it and Sir John agrees; then withdraw before he has time to grow tired of you.

She was perhaps nine years old when he died. It can scarcely have been a significant personal loss to her. Quite likely she did not realize for some time what a massive change the old knight's death would make to all of her family.

Perhaps for a few days there were more comings and goings than usual at the Pastons' Norwich house. Then the place emptied out for Sir John's funeral, which was held at the monastery of St Benet, a few miles west of Caister. John Paston, cast in his self-designated role as chief mourner, took care to bring a very large entourage.[1] Margery's big brothers would have been among those who went, and so would the family's men of business and their servants. Margery herself probably did not go: funerals were not seen in those days as appropriate occasions for young girls, and in some country parts no women attended them at all. But there was much to do surrounding the service, and everyone who could help must have been expected to do so. Eighteen banners and dozens of pennants were to be flown, far more than the Paston and Fastolf households put together would have possessed. Scores of black gowns were run up for the mourners. Animals had to be killed for the funeral feast, loaves baked and beer brewed. William Worcester supervised some of this activity, and placed many of the orders, but Margaret Paston must have been at full stretch too. Quite likely Margery was taken down to Mautby with her mother and the other young children in the family, and sat down to work along with every other woman and girl capable of holding a needle.

It was early November of 1459 when Fastolf died, and by the time the funeral was over it was pushing on towards Christmas. The Paston children and their mother headed back to Norwich, but their father did not come home. The family must have missed him. Although John Paston was away for most of the time, he normally made a point of being with his wife and children over Christmas. And they needed him particularly, because Margaret Paston was edgy and uncertain, and looking for information and reassurance.

She had to get it from John II and John III, as did Margery herself. Her brothers were grown up now, seventeen and fifteen, old enough to stand with the men. John II was an intelligent lad who seems to have had a great deal of shy charm. He was fond of books, and of having a good time. His father appears not to have involved him in all the practical activity over Fastolf's death, and since he had a lazy streak, perhaps he did not exactly beg to play a part. His uncle Clement was barely older than him, but Clement belonged very firmly to a different generation: he was part of the family enterprise, in a way that the young Johns were not. Perhaps Uncle William had played a hand there.

John III was a less flamboyant character, more steady in temperament, not averse to following in his brother's footsteps.

What Margery's mother might have been slow to tell her, her brothers would have passed on soon enough. Their father was Sir John Fastolf's heir. He was to have Caister Castle, Sir John's house in Norwich, his mansion in Southwark, his estates in Norfolk and Suffolk: the lot. He had to set up a college of monks, but that was the only restriction on him. (Oh, and he had to get the old knight's will proven. His sons might not have realized yet that this would be no formality.) What did this mean? Why, that they were rich! They would live in the huge new castle, and dine off silver. They would meet the king and the duke of York. (Not both at once, mind, with the country at war.) Margery might go to court herself one day; she would marry a rich man, perhaps even a lord. Well, that was optimistic, since she was no heiress, but even so, she would marry well. They must not crow, not in public: but in private the boys must have been jubilant, and Margery thrilled too at all that she learned.

John II could look to go to court now, and become a knight and courtier. The boys could fight in tournaments, perhaps fight in battles too. And there were battles to fight, in those days: a couple of them that summer past, between supporters of King Henry and his queen, and supporters of the duke of York. However their parents were anxious that the family keep clear of such troublesome activity, and did not encourage their sons to go to war.

The war had not come to Norwich, but it was not far from touching distance, and the funeral, with its great gathering of the Pastons and their associates, must have made it seem much closer. Perhaps John Paston senior had no plans to become a knight, and Christopher Hanson and the rest of Fastolf's men had passed their fighting days, but Aunt Elizabeth's new husband was very definitely involved.

Robert Poynings must have seemed an exciting character to the Paston lads, and probably to Margery too. He had been sword-bearer to Jack Cade, at his shoulder throughout the rebellion of 1450, and hard pressed to escape when it fell apart. He had intervened gallantly when one of Fastolf's men had been captured spying on the rebels, and some of Cade's men had suggested killing him: he had spoken up for the man, ensured he was not harmed, and gained much gratitude from Fastolf's household.[2] He had been accused of robberies, and locked up in the Tower of London – but had been tried and found not guilty, which proved (to his family at least) that it was all wicked false accusations by his enemies. And he was politically active: while John Paston senior and his brothers stayed carefully neutral, Poynings spoke of fighting for the duke of York, trying to ensure the country was governed differently and better. Nor would he stop at speaking, that was clear: he was a man who would ride off and join the duke's army.

Margery's mother would have given short shrift to any romanticizing of this history, though. Her main concern at this time was that her family should behave in a way that could provoke no criticism. The rules she had lived by all her life were those of the comfortable gentry classes, and she did not know how people who lived in large castles conducted themselves. She told her eldest son to go and ask for advice from Lady Morley, the widowed sister of the late duke of Suffolk. How should they behave over Christmas in a house of mourning for a distant but (in the circumstances) extremely important relative?

John probably grumbled at this thoroughly embarrassing task. Could they not guess at what to do? Would anyone know if they got it wrong behind their closed doors? He went on the errand, even so, and came back with Lady Morley's firm instructions. No fancy dress, no music: no harps, no lutes, no singing. No 'lewd sports'. The family might play tables (a form of backgammon), and chess and cards, but there should be no entertainment more boisterous than that.[3]

John probably did not like this advice any more than he had liked obtaining it. Perhaps he had a hand in encouraging his mother to check again. He ensured that this time it was his brother who had to go visiting and questioning. Lady Stapleton, another of the grandes dames of Norwich, was consulted next. Lady Morley is right, she said, not surprisingly. It ought to be a quiet Christmas, with plenty of prayer.

During the quiet Christmas in mourning, during the hours on her knees in church, Margery must have noticed some curious glances. All the Paston children, and the servants, would have been told not just what to do, but what to say to anyone who

Chapel of St Nicholas, Gipping, Suffolk

questioned them. If anyone asked about a quarrel between their father and Judge Yelverton, they were to say they knew nothing about it.[4] If anyone said, was it true that Sir John Fastolf did not leave a will, they were to say, of course it was not true. He had left a nuncupative will. This was a word that must have become very familiar to them all. It meant, not a formal written will, but an oral declaration, sworn to in the presence of witnesses. They could point out that their father was a lawyer, and that his advice on the subject could be relied on. This might be an unusual situation, but a nuncupative will, witnessed by men of good reputation (of whom John Paston had been one) was perfectly valid. There was no doubt that it reflected what Fastolf had intended. He had said again and again that he wished John Paston senior to be his heir.

There was no doubt for Margery and her siblings, perhaps. But even a child of nine or ten would have noticed that not everyone in Norwich shared this attitude.

Margery surely knew Samson and Hercules House, the great mansion that Sir John had owned in Norwich, simply because everyone beyond infancy who lived in Norwich would have known the place. It was opposite the church of St James Pockthorpe, in the east of the city, a good walk from St Peter Hungate and Elm Hill. Fastolf seems not to have come there often, so perhaps she had never been into the house. The Pastons had every right to go there, indeed to live there if they wished, if the house had been left to them. But the will was not proven yet, and it was apparent already that they could not afford to antagonize anyone who might have a hand in the process of proving it. There were Fastolf's nephews, who might have expected to inherit themselves. There was Judge Yelverton, who had been named as one of many executors in drafts of Fastolf's will – and Margery's father's row with him about which the Pastons were definitely not talking. There were all their old enemies, the men who had supported the rival claimants to their family estates.

So they did not move in to Samson and Hercules House, though perhaps Margery, with her brothers and her mother, risked a look around the place. It had a Great Hall with stained glass windows, with images of St Margaret, St John the Baptist in a camel skin, the Virgin Mary, St Blaise holding a wool comb, and St Catherine. In the large north window there was a row of ten life-sized statues of warriors: David with his sling, Samson with his lion skin, Hercules with his club, and others they might have found harder to identify.[5] It was eccentric, imposing, Fastolffian – not Pastonian, not yet at least.

Perhaps she was beginning to realize now just how much things had changed.

There were some sizeable Fastolf estates just outside the city too. Margery is perhaps less likely to have visited them at this point, but her big brothers surely did, and reported back. At Hellesdon and Drayton there were houses big enough to be called castles, though they were more on the lines of the derelict castle at Gresham than of Caister itself. Brick at Drayton, stone at Hellesdon. Lots of land, mills on the River Wensum, and herds of sheep. Will we live there, she might have asked her mother? The answer this time would have been more positive. Yes, we shall spend time there. Her mother might not have added, we must do so, but Margery's brothers would certainly have realized that this was true. The family needed to drive home (without being ostentatious) the message that all of this was now theirs.

A Norfolk winter. Stark-twigged trees in dank forests. Bleak ploughed fields where no crops grew. Sheep and cows penned tight, their grazing lands left thin-grassed and empty. Blackened, rotting weeds at the edge of the fishponds and rivers. Thin spirals of smoke from the chimneys of low-set cottages. Death and decay, and barely yet a hint of the coming spring.

Damp wood and a squelch underfoot in the barges that plyed the Pickerill Fleet. At one end of the channel, the familiar comforts of Mautby Hall, reed-thatched, crouched amid woodland and fishponds; at the other, the brash red brick of Caister Castle, a huge tall-towered edifice set in a wide moat.

And the Paston family, come to explore what had now become theirs.

Even if they had visited many times before, still it must have been strange and exciting to be greeted by the servants who were now their servants, to go through the great gate that was now their great gate, and into the courtyard that was now theirs. It was all theirs. The monks were to have some of the income, true, and needed somewhere to live, but a small college of monks did not fill a great castle; they could be corralled into one wing, or perhaps a separate place could be erected for them.

John Paston had had an inventory of Fastolf's possessions drawn up, probably by William Worcester and Fastolf's clerk, Thomas Howes. It runs to just under twenty-four pages of small type in an Edwardian edition of the Paston letters.[6] Margaret Paston might have had a copy, and checked over it with her older children as they went from room to room, and room, and room.

So many rooms. The buttery, the great chamber, the White Chamber, the chamber with hanging cloths portraying shepherds, the yeoman's chamber for strangers, the white-hangings chamber next to the Wardrobe, the chamber over the draught bridge, the middle chamber, and more, and more. The chapel had vestments, missals, a psalter clasped with silver; in the kitchen were great brass pots, ladles and skimmers, a brass mortar with a pestle, pot hooks and a vinegar bottle. There were tapestries on the walls, feather beds, blankets and down pillows in the bedrooms. Margery and her brothers must have marvelled at Fastolf's wardrobe – his gown of cloth of gold, his 'broken gown of sanguine', his gown of French russet lined with black cloth, several other gowns, thirteen different jackets and doublets. Perhaps they were not quite the size, or the style, to suit her brothers, but they could be altered, and the boys might both have acquired some of these good rich clothes. They would have admired 'the bed in the great stable', three great steel crossbows, plus other crossbows, quarrels to shoot from them, suits of armour; in the cellar, 'certain vessels which John Ouresby is charged with' (by an indenture, a copy attached to the list), plus plenty of good French wine.

The gold and silver was astonishing. Each piece had been carefully weighed and described: a pair of basins, all gilt, with an antelope in the middle, weighing 1,100 ounces; two ewers, gilt, pounced with flowers and branches, weighing 39 ounces; a spice plate, well gilt like a double rose, my master's helmet in the middle, with red roses of my master's arms, weighing 510 ounces, and more, and more. John Paston might have been secretive about the money that Fastolf had left (the money his brothers had helped him spirit safely away from prying eyes), but one could hardly be secretive about such strutting, confident, eloquent silver and gold.

In the middle of winter no sane man would dine in the arctic wastes of the great hall, but there were rooms designed for cold-weather use, lower-ceilinged, with tapestries to warm the brick, where good big fires could be lit in the grates. If much of the silver had been locked up for safety, they might have kept some back to gleam in the light of the candles.

The light flickered, and Margery's mother continued to be uncharacteristically nervous. Perhaps Margery herself had a sense of the reasons. It was so much; it was too much. The older Pastons knew already what it was like to hear the wolves barking. There would be packs of them now, yapping at the doors. The family might never be fully confident that all this would remain theirs.

Church of St Nicholas,
Oakley, Suffolk

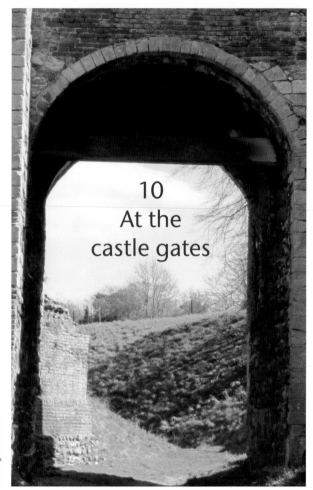

10
At the castle gates

Framlingham Castle

A year and a half later, in June 1461, Richard Calle went to Framlingham. It was probably his first visit for some time, since the Pastons had kept him extremely busy since Fastolf had died.[1]

He perhaps went first to the shop. His father had probably returned to Great Waldingfield by this time – he seems to have died there the following year, so he might well have been in failing health at this time – but Richard's brother John would have been in Framlingham running the shop, and perhaps others of his family were there as well. John had married, and by this time he might have had children (he was to have two sons who survived infancy, Robert and Nicholas). Of course Richard wanted to see his family and catch up with their news, but he had other reasons too for heading to the shop. He had a difficult task ahead of him, and his brother's local knowledge might help him in planning his approach to it.

The duke of Norfolk had sent his men to occupy Caister Castle.

This was a disaster for the Paston family, and it was scarcely less of a disaster for the Calles. John, Richard and all their family prided themselves on their good relations with the duke. If the duke and the Pastons were at odds, then John Calle would inevitably take the duke's side, but he would have realized that Richard badly wanted them not to be at odds, and that his objective in coming to Framlingham was to try to mend relations, not to make the rift worse. So Richard could trust his brother to help him as much as he could, without risking his own good standing with the duke.

The family business done – the babies kissed, news of relatives and friends exchanged – the two brothers probably sat down together and shared all they knew about this miserable business.

This action of the duke's had not thundered down from a cloudless sky. It was not so much the cause as the result of a rift that had built up. There were several reasons for it.

One was that the duke clearly shared the general opinion that John Paston senior had not proved his right to Fastolf's estates, and as likely as not never would, for the simple reason that he had no such right. The unsigned will was just not sufficient to justify overlooking the man's nearest heirs and passing his property to a man whose main qualification for receiving it was that he had been responsible for drawing up said will. John senior claimed to have witnesses that it had been Fastolf's intention to leave the estate to him, but even to a man who did not trouble with the finer details of the story, it was clear that he did not have the universal support of everyone involved. Fastolf's own servants were at best only passively on his side. (This was not least, as Richard knew, because they had still not been granted the small inheritances they had expected, which had not been mentioned in the nuncupative will.) Some of the executors the old knight had named were standing back, but others were adamant that John senior's claim was entirely unjustified. Judge Yelverton was prominent among them.

Plenty of people would have liked to acquire some or all of Fastolf's property, and the duke of Norfolk was one of them. He could dress up his action as support to one of the other claimed heirs (that is, Fastolf's nephews), but at the core of it was his hope that Caister would fall permanently into his own hands. He would

Church of St Andrew, Bedingham, Norfolk

have to pay something for the title, since he had no claim otherwise, but he seems to have been quite willing to do so in order to acquire this prime Norfolk property, arguably the finest new castle in the entire country.

Second was a feud between John senior and one of the duke's young kinsmen, John Howard.[2] Both men had wanted to be nominated the county of Norfolk's representative to Parliament, and they had clashed at the Shire Day in Norwich when the election took place. One of Howard's servants had struck Paston twice with a dagger. Fortunately he had been wearing a padded doublet, so the knife had not wounded him. And whatever the rights and wrongs of the row, Howard's servant should not have struck him. But that did not disguise the fact that it had been stupid of him to challenge the duke's man for the nomination, and more stupid to let the challenge degenerate into a fight. It also reminded people uncomfortably of other fights that John senior had got himself into (not least, the one that had seen Judge Yelverton's servant end up dead). True, it might have been a good thing in a political sense for John senior to get the nomination, which could have strengthened his position in the upper reaches of Norfolk society, but that was far outweighed by the bad effects of this public brawl.

Third, and not insignificant, was the national political situation. Things were looking good for the duke of Norfolk at that time, the kind of good that gave him the confidence to throw his weight about. He had brought his men to the battle of Towton a couple of months earlier just in time to turn the fight in favour of Edward of York (the young son of the now dead duke of York), and now that Edward was on the brink of being crowned as king of England, Norfolk was high in his favour.

The Pastons had not fought at Towton. Robert Poynings, Elizabeth's husband, had fought for York at the battle of St Albans a few months earlier, but it had cost him his life, and dead men could hardly call in favours. Not fighting at all was better than having fought for the wrong side, but when many men had risked their lives to see Edward brought to the throne, the Pastons could not expect to stand at the front of the crowd after having made no efforts at all.

So if the duke of Norfolk was not entirely justified in occupying Caister, he had reason to think that he could get away with occupying Caister, and indeed with making his occupation permanent.

What could Richard Calle argue against this? Nothing, really. Or at best, next to nothing. He could try to convince himself that Fastolf really had intended John Paston senior to be his heir. Though not as likely as Paston made it out to be, it was not incredible: there was the connection of sorts through Margaret Paston, there was the genuine fondness of the old knight for Paston, and there was his notable lack of enthusiasm for the other candidates. But as like as not Richard had not even convinced himself fully of this – although he was pragmatic enough to continue to work for the Pastons – and that made it unlikely he would convince the duke of Norfolk, especially when it was in the duke's clear interest to be unconvinced.

Also, he was the wrong person to be making the appeal, and he surely knew it. His family's connection with the duke was not an advantage here, because he was hobbled by his anxiety to not damage that connection. And he was not John Paston. As any man could have seen (John Calle not least), if John Paston senior really wanted to mend his relations with the duke, he should have come to Framlingham himself, with something to offer, and not sent his estate manager empty-handed.

John Calle probably gave his brother two useful pieces of information. First, the man who headed the duke's little troop of men at Caister, one Fitzwilliam, was at that very time with the duke in Framlingham Castle. And second, Thomas Fastolf was in town.

This Fastolf was one of Sir John's nephews, and the man who many thought should have been the main heir to Sir John's estates. He had been building up support for his case over the previous months, and a legal hearing in Norfolk had pronounced him the rightful heir.[3] According to John Paston senior the inquisition had not been properly drawn up (it should have had a royal summons, but it had not), but that did not alter the fact that many men had heard its findings, and given some weight to them.

The duke of Norfolk was one of them. And the logical deduction from Fastolf's presence in Framlingham was that he and the duke were looking to come to a deal which would leave Norfolk sitting happy at Caister, and Fastolf getting much, if not all, of the rest of his uncle's estate.

Richard probably considered whether he should approach Thomas Fastolf, but realistically there was no benefit for him in doing so. Even if he had been authorized to negotiate with the man (he clearly was not), he could not have afforded to bid for his favour against the duke. He might also have considered whether it was worth talking to Fitzwilliam. It was not. His main conclusion was probably that it was bad news that both men were with the duke. Fastolf would reinforce the duke's conviction that John senior had not genuinely inherited the estate, and Fitzwilliam would pass on every little gripe and groan from the now thoroughly grumpy old Fastolf men at Caister.

Was there anyone else he could talk to? His brother suggested Richard Southwell. One of the duke's retainers, Southwell had had business dealings with the Pastons over many years. He too was in Framlingham (a crowded place at this time), and would probably be reasonably well disposed towards the Paston cause – or at least if he was not, Richard would be the wiser for knowing it. So when he left the grocer's shop it was to seek out Southwell at one of the local inns.

Richard wrote later to John senior to report on all he had done at Framlingham, but he was pretty brief on the subject of what he and Southwell said to each other.[1] The main thing that comes across is that the meeting did not go well. Arguably he

Church of St Mary the Virgin, Wilby, Norfolk

would have done better not even to tell his master this much, but he presumably felt he had to show that he had made every effort. Also, this was perhaps something he felt John senior needed to know. John senior was not good at absorbing the reactions of others. At this time, Richard probably thought he was far too optimistic about his prospects, and far too reluctant to negotiate with the men who might have done a deal that would leave him with a decent share of the Fastolf estate. John senior probably assumed that men like Southwell fully accepted the rightness of his cause. It would have been better for him if he had taken it in that they did not.

So Richard passed on that Southwell thought John senior 'strangely disposed' and believed that he 'trusted no man'.[4] Perhaps he thought himself that this was too harsh a judgement, and even though he was more realistic than his master, perhaps he was genuinely surprised by the depth of Southwell's hostility. The two men ended up trading bitter words.

Not good. Details of this argument too would trundle up the hill to the castle.

So by the time he presented himself at the castle gate, Richard knew he could not possibly get a kindly reception. But a mission is a mission, and Richard was a diligent man, and one who would have to report back to his master. He showed the gateman his letters, and asked if he might present them to the duke – or failing that, to his chamberlain, or another of his senior servants. The answer was no. His letters were taken, and he was told someone would be in touch.

He retreated back to the town, since it was apparent no billet in the castle was likely to be provided for him, and must have stayed overnight with his brother and his family. These were good honest people who had no claims to have inherited a fortune on the basis of an unsigned will. We must hope he had a good time.

Word came, in some roundabout way, that Southwell had been sent for by the duke. Then one of the duke's servants came in search of Richard. The first question he had was, where was Richard's master?

Richard said, 'He's with the king.' It sounded good. It must have had a smidgen of truth in it. John Paston senior was not in the king's service, and all the duke's men surely knew that. But his eldest son was now hanging around Westminster, hoping to find a position at court, and John senior himself was sending plenty of petitions to the king.

This got an answer that it perhaps deserved. The message came from the castle, in that case the duke will reply to these letters direct to the king. The messenger added that Southwell would be responsible for reporting to Westminster.

This was bad enough news that Richard felt he had to try to patch things up with

Bedesmen, from a brass in St Stephen's Church, Norwich

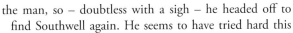

the man, so – doubtless with a sigh – he headed off to find Southwell again. He seems to have tried hard this time to avoid arguing with him. He needed to learn what the man would say to the king, and he managed to do so. Southwell told him that he and the duke – in some combination – reckoned that some of the points John senior had made in his letters were untrue, and they would report this. He told Richard too that Thomas Fastolf and a couple of other men had delivered to the duke 'certain evidence' to back up their claims to the Fastolf estates. King Edward would be shown this evidence as well.

The other thing Richard learned, perhaps over a mug of ale at the inn, was that the duke had left only a handful of men to guard Caister. So it might have been possible to wrest it back. But then, if John senior had wanted to completely wreck what remained of his reputation in Norfolk and Suffolk, he could hardly have done better than to send his men to turn the duke of Norfolk's troops out of a castle that many men believed was not his true property.

Still, Richard probably reckoned that the chances of John senior acting on this information, if he were given it, were little more than zero. When had the man ever pressed his claims in person, except in the lawcourts? It was his wife, or his estate servants, or even his chaplain – it might soon be his sons – whom he sent to the front line. All those individuals had more sense than to pick an even larger argument with the duke.

He had to write something positive, to balance out the warnings about Southwell. So he suggested that 'saving your better advice' it would be wise for the Pastons to marshall their own evidence of their claims, and have it ready to counter the evidences that Southwell's man was bringing, and he added a note about the vulnerability of the castle. He phrased it only slightly cryptically: 'if you think it best to etc., send word and I suppose a remedy shall be had'.[5]

Privately, he surely realized that it would not be remotely as easy as this implied to improve the situation. So he headed back to Norwich, sent his letter from there, and waited for further instructions.

Church of St Mary the Virgin, Saxlingham Nethergate, Norfolk

11
Hell's
den

Although the Pastons had spent some time at Caister, they do not seem to have lived there in the months before the duke of Norfolk took it from them. So to Margery, its loss was a second-hand one: they would simply not be going there for a while. Only a while, her parents must have insisted to their family, their servants, their friends: the duke of Norfolk had no right to the place, and in time that would be accepted by the courts, and he would have to give it back.

They had been thrown out of Gresham and later got it back, so this was not beyond belief.

But that was the point: it had happened at Gresham, a troop of armed men shoving the Pastons out of a house and lands that they claimed to be theirs. And now it was happening all over again, and not just at Caister. The duke of Suffolk (son of the one murdered a decade earlier) was becoming powerful in the region, and a patron of the men, or the sons of the men, who had backed Lord Moleyns at Gresham: a nasty gang, notorious for operating with impunity, stealing and conning their way into other people's property. Suffolk had an estate outside Norwich at Costessey, and he made it clear he would like to add Fastolf's old lands at Drayton and Hellesdon to it. At Dedham in Essex, things had gone further: Suffolk's men had already moved onto the land and were busily collecting the rent. Meanwhile Judge Yelverton and his cronies were trying to grab Cotton in Suffolk. The duke of Exeter had his eye on Fastolf's house in Southwark. Another man was claiming Stratton in Norfolk. John Paston senior could not write fast enough to draw up all the petitions he needed to lodge.

If Margery's father trusted no one and started at shadows, this was not insanity. It was because he was surrounded by powerful enemies, whose successes emboldened other men to join them. His wife was less suspicious by nature, less inclined to act 'strange', but in these days she was counting over her friends, watching warily for her enemies, and ordering her children to take extra care each time they left the house.

We shall be rich. Perhaps they were. But the greatest change over the previous two years in Margery's life was probably the increase in her family not of affluence, but of fear.

And of notoriety, too. The Christmas after Fastolf's death, the family must have thought the half-heard mutters outside church after mass, the men crossing the street to avoid talking to them, the awkward questions – all the things that made it uncomfortable to venture out in Norwich – would be temporary, and that within months, or perhaps a year at most, the will would be proved, John senior's holdings confirmed, their new and higher situation established as a fact and accepted by those around them. This had not happened, though. The tactics they were trying to make it happen did not seem to be working. Richard Calle's trip to Framlingham was just one in a series of failed attempts to make things come right.

Margery herself was too young to tell whether any of this was her father's fault, or even to appreciate that it might be. She was probably not aware of some of the threats, and although she must have been aware of others, they perhaps did not seem to her worse than the threats that other people faced. In some ways, indeed, they were not. These were lawless times, and even someone with the knowledge and skill to analyse John Paston's actions would have been pushed to differentiate between the trouble he had brought on his family, the troubles caused by the houses of York and Lancaster and their supporters, and the kind of random trouble even the most cautious man might be unfortunate enough to walk into. It was not only the Pastons who were afraid in these days: most people were, and had reason to be.

What Margery had seen must have included her father coming home with his doublet ripped after the fight at the Guildhall on Shire Day. Later that year the wife of the coroner of Norfolk turned up on their doorstep. This was a family her own knew well. The coroner had been dragged from his house and killed, the family's goods ransacked and stolen; his wife was hysterical and in despair. Margaret Paston, not a woman known for her open-handedness, gave her 6s 8d to help her out.[1]

Margery knew of Aunt Elizabeth's husband dying in the war, although most people probably did not then think of it as a war, and no one called it by the name we know now, the Wars of the Roses. She probably knew that afterwards Aunt Elizabeth had been thrown out of her own house by her husband's relatives, left facing destitution with her baby son, and that her brothers (William and Clement: she did not turn to John) had had to give her emergency help and find her lodgings.

A messenger came that July from the group of monks at Caister. (John senior had not yet obtained the licence for Fastolf's college, but he had recruited some monks, presumably to prove to his critics that he was fulfilling Fastolf's intentions.) They had not been turned out of their lodgings in the castle by the duke of Norfolk's men, but their possessions had been ransacked, and they were being watched day and night.[2]

It was not just to face out the duke of Suffolk's men that the family spent much of their time living outside Norwich, on the old Fastolf estate at Hellesdon. It was also because the city was a dangerous place, and their house at Hellesdon was a sturdy one, all but a castle, and farther removed from the risk of violence.

Hellesdon sits in the valley of the meandering River Wensum, to the west of the city of Norwich. It was known for its rabbit warrens, and for the water mills that had been located on the manor probably since Saxon times, as the muddle of pools and mill races along the valley floor testified. The old mill and the new mill of Margery's time (Hellesdon men saw no reason to be imaginative in naming them) were probably dual-purpose mills, used for both grinding corn and fulling cloth. The corn came from farms around the city, and the flour it made went to the Norwich markets. The cloth came from the city itself. So there was a well-trodden road from Hellesdon into Norwich, following the river up to the leper house, the city wall and St Augustine's Gate. Drayton was to the north-west; Costessey, the duke of Suffolk's estate, lay over the river to the south.

Hellesdon village was set on a low hill that rose above the river, focused around the church of St Mary, a little flint and stone building with a bell cote – it might grandly have been called a steeple – to hold the bell that the lord of the manor had donated a century before. Margery would have gone often to the church, and perhaps she and her brothers and sister were allowed to roam the fields, fisheries and warrens of the home farm. Men were employed to tend to the stew ponds where fish were raised for food, and there was a warreners' lodge, where the men who caught the rabbits based themselves. That July the warrens produced 1,100 rabbits that were sent down to London for sale.[3]

The house the Pastons knew at Hellesdon is long gone, but it seems to have been a rectangular stone building, with a great hall and a chamber above it. There was a buttery, where the food supplies were kept, and also the dining equipment: salt cellars, candlesticks, cloths and towels; and a kitchen – probably a separate building – which held among other things equipment for salting meat, and an axe for chopping the wood for the fire. There was room for the servants as well as the family to live, including a room that they called the chantry, which Richard Calle at some point used as his quarters.[4] Among the outbuildings was a brewhouse, with skips for holding the barley, and equipment for drying it to produce the malt that was the core ingredient of ale; mash tuns for the brewing process, and barrels to hold the ale once brewed. (The Pastons did not see themselves as innkeepers, and they probably did not sell their ale, even if it was brewed on quite a large scale: it was for the family, their servants and perhaps tenants in the neighbourhood.)

The family here in 1461 consisted of Margery's mother, and less often her father; her sister Anne, her young brothers Edmund and Walter when they were not at school, and the runt of the family, William, then aged two or so. John III seems also to have been mostly at home in this period, helping their mother with her business affairs.

When Margaret Paston was in the city she would have transacted her business there, but when she stayed at Hellesdon the estate servants who reported to her came out to the house, so Margery and her family got to know not just the household servants, but these men too. There were more of them now, since there were so many estates to be run, and so many difficulties to be contended with. Richard Calle was a familiar face, and the new generation of servants included John Pamping, who worked particularly closely with John senior, effectively as his personal servant as well as handling much of his liaison with his wife, and John Daubeney – Daube to his friends – who seems to have been a noisy, cheerful type. He had perhaps been a soldier before joining the family, and played a prominent part in ensuring their security. Father Gloys spent time at Hellesdon too, and there would have been visits from the tenant farmers.

One of the farms at Drayton, Fairchilds, had been promised by Sir John Fastolf to William Worcester, and quite likely Worcester came up to the area occasionally to pursue his claim. He never gave up, though it took him a good fifteen years to obtain his house.

Grandma Paston did not live at Hellesdon, but in her house in Norwich, or at times at Oxnead and Paston, so the family saw her, but not frequently. Margery must have seen little or nothing, though, of the London-based Pastons, her uncles William and Clement (neither of whom had yet married) and her aunt Elizabeth. John II was not at Hellesdon either. He was in London, and it was clear by now that he hoped to spend much of his time there and at Westminster, fulfilling his ambition to join the king's court.

The River Wensum at Hellesdon, Norfolk

Hellesdon did not have the grandeur of Caister, but the manor house was well equipped and must have been comfortable. Some of Fastolf's possessions from Caister had probably followed Margaret Paston west, and there was silver to grace the table, and good food to eat from it. Complain as Margaret might from time to time, the family wore good clothes in rich fabrics, and rode good horses. This was not deer country – there were no chases, just warrens and sheep fields – but they kept hawks, and went out to hunt with them.

King Edward was crowned by the archbishop of Canterbury that June. John II and his father, down in London, would have seen the great processions and celebrations that accompanied the coronation. On the whole life at Hellesdon must have been on the quiet side, so Margery and the other children would have been impatient for someone to come from London and tell them all about the festivities.

There was hope here, real hope. People prayed that now King Edward had replaced the daft old king Henry, he would bring stability and firm governance to the country, and the Pastons in particular hoped that if John II could establish himself at court and make useful contacts, it would help to ensure that the family's petitions were heard, the Fastolf will proved, and their own situation made secure.

Margery's father was the first to come back to Norfolk, in August. Margery cannot have seen him for a while, and she might well have been shaken by his appearance and his manner. The stress of working to secure the Fastolf estates had aged him, and made him suspicious and irritable.[5] They must all have hoped that the peace of Hellesdon would have a calming effect on him.

And it might have seemed at first that this would happen. Supervising the first of the harvest, eating the fish from the ponds, roasted rabbit and the ripe fruit from the garden;

riding across the water meadows in the August sunshine; telling his family tales of the pageants and masses to welcome the new king: all this was stuff to soothe an exhausted lawyer fresh from London. Then a servant called Peacock, who had been assigned to John II, arrived at Hellesdon Hall.

His news was for Margery's parents, not for her and the other children. They probably learned first of the outcome: that John II was to be called home. And they would have realized when they were told this, even if they had not heard the raised voices that preceded the announcement, that their parents had quarrelled bitterly over it. In a family known for its squabbles and feuds, this

Church of St Mary, Shelton, Norfolk

was rare and unnerving: their mother normally supported their father in all the decisions that he made. But she found it hard to stomach this one, that was clear.

John III probably found out the rest – more likely from Peacock than from his mother – and told the younger children some at least of it. John II was likely to be even more upset than his mother when he got the summons, because he had been hoping to travel with the king's household into Wales. He had suffered, though, from the usual predicament of Paston men: a chronic shortage of money. He had told Peacock to go to his uncle Clement, and ask him to send to Christopher Hanson (the steward at Fastolf's old house in Southwark), who, he hoped, would provide both a hundred shillings and the horse harness which he had left to be cleaned.

Clement had understandably wanted to know more before getting involved, and had guessed too that Hanson could not provide that much money, so he was all too likely to be leaned on himself for an advance. So he had questioned Peacock, who had told him he reckoned John II's request was reasonable. Although he had spent the money his father had already forwarded him, that was not through profligacy, but because the costs in the king's household were higher than John senior had expected. Peacock had added, though, that John II was still struggling to get established in the royal household. He did not know many people beyond his first contact (one John Weeks, an usher in the king's chamber), and had not yet had his promised introduction to the king. And he was not listed by the stewards as one of the household members, which meant that he was not being fed in the hall.

Clement had decided the best thing to do was to write to John senior, and ask for his instructions. But when Peacock had gone back to John II and told him this, his master had flown into a rage and dismissed him. What was more, he had sent him back to Norfolk with a long letter, in which he had not only assured his father he was working hard to get established at court, but had complained about Peacock. He 'is not for me', John II had written. 'God send grace that he may do you good service, but by my estimation it is not likely.'[6] Although Peacock had dutifully delivered this letter, he had probably guessed it was critical of him, and John senior's questions to him would have confirmed that. So it was hardly surprising he had not been complimentary about John II in return.

It might have been better for John II if Clement's letter had preceded Peacock, but more likely it followed him, since it was written a couple of days later. Though Clement related John II's problems at court, he also pointed out the drawbacks of withdrawing him, including how it would look to the king and his courtiers. Those were probably the points that his mother had made to his father. And there was justice in them: this was a time when the Pastons needed to build some influence with the king, even if it did prove slower and more costly than they might have hoped. But John senior had made up his mind by then, and he was not willing to change it.

All pictures: Church of St Miles Coslany, Norwich

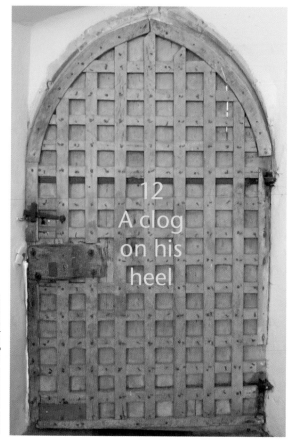

12

A clog on his heel

Church of All Saints, Edingthorpe, Norfolk

It is not easy for any outsider working in a family enterprise when a new generation comes to join it. Richard Calle had weathered the upheaval of the Pastons taking over the Fastolf estates, the influx of new servants, and kept his position as their main man of business. He had seen young John III come to work with his mother, and adapted to the shift in relations, seemingly unperturbed. But it probably suited him that John II showed no inclination to join the team in East Anglia managing the Paston/Fastolf lands. Perhaps he had a provincial disdain for courtiers who thought themselves far more important than they deserved to be, but it was in many ways in his interest for John Paston's heir to become one of them.

It was not all bad news that John II had come back to Norfolk at this point, though. There were so many fronts on which storms were brewing, and just as John senior was hard pushed, even with help from his brothers, to keep up with the legal actions that were called for, so Richard and his team were stretched to get around all the estates, reassure all the tenants, keep the rent collection up to date, the stray wood gathered for kindling and the old trees felled, the crops sold, the sheep sheared and slaughtered, the manor courts held and judgments given that all could accept, and do all the rest that needed to be done to ensure they were in the best possible position to resist challenges to their authority. Whatever John II claimed, it did not look as if he had achieved much at court. Perhaps he could achieve more by riding around the family lands and pitching into the business of managing them.

The bad news – the really bad news – was that John senior had embarked on a feud with his eldest son. He had scarcely patched up the old feud with his brothers, and here he was, at loggerheads with the next generation.

Richard probably reckoned it was not all John senior's fault. He might be suspicious, awkward and temperamentally at odds with his son, but if he thought John II indolent, it was most likely because he was. Certainly he was very different from the sober and thoughtful Clement, even though they were the same age. Whatever the rights and wrongs of the money he had spent at court, Richard might also have shared his father's view that the lad was a spendthrift. He was shaping up to be a womanizer too, and if those with that fault are typically blessed with charm, they still cause the women involved plenty of pain. But regardless of the reasons and justifications, this feud was one the Paston family could not afford.

So Richard seems to have done his best to soften its edges. John II might be livid that he had been yanked out of Westminster and dumped in dreary Hellesdon, but he would have less time to dwell on the insult if he was kept busy. John senior might think his son a wastrel who had achieved nothing so far and probably never would, but he would have to temper his view if the lad actually made himself useful. Richard's role here was clear: he needed to give the boy a hand-up, guide him in a direction that would suit his talents, and if and when he proved some use, make sure his father knew all about it.

John II had strength and energy and at least some sense. Not all the men who acted for the Pastons can have enjoyed the rough end of their work: coming down heavily on tenants behind with their rent, distraining their goods, facing up to the duke of Suffolk's thugs. But John II had something of his mother in him as well as his father, seemed to enjoy a degree of danger, and might yet prove to have a talent for the work. His mother was probably happy to back up Richard's suggestion that he leave his young brother to work in the counting house, and head out into the countryside with the estate team.

Church of St Mary, Shelton, Norfolk

They had scarcely embarked on this strategy, though – perhaps had not had time to embark on it at all – when a new crisis struck the family.

News of it came in another letter from Clement, written from London 'at midnight'.[1] When he received it, John senior acted as urgently as his younger brother had done in writing: he set off immediately.

That kind of frantic response generates waves: everyone at Hellesdon would have known where he had gone, and why. The king had issued two summonses against him, both of them prompted by complaints from John Howard, backed up by the duke of Norfolk, the duke of Suffolk and a host of other men. It was a disaster that he had not replied to either of them. Now a third summons was threatening him with death if he did not present himself at court immediately.

The duke of Norfolk. Norfolk's kinsman Howard. The duke of Suffolk, and other men too. Men who, some of them at least, were in 'great fellowship'[2] with the king, in a perfect position to whisper poison in his ear. It would have been no wonder if John II complained loudly to anyone who would listen that this would not have happened if he had still been at court. His father was perilously long on enemies and short on influential friends, and what he had done but thrown away the fragile toehold his son had established at Westminster? The result was that allegations against him were listened to first, and acted on second, and the answers he might have made to them were heard not at all.

They must all have waited anxiously for more news to come. Had John senior arrived at Westminster in time to answer the summons? And when a messenger arrived, the information he brought would have blown round the manor like an autumn gale. John Paston had been met in London by officers at law who had escorted him to the Fleet prison.

Being jailed in these days was not a sentence for a crime, albeit it must have felt like a punishment. Men who could not pay their debts, or against whom charges had been laid, were held in the cells till they could be tried in a hearing known as a jail delivery, at which if they were found guilty, a sentence – not itself of imprisonment – was passed on them. The deliveries were held regularly, though never soon enough for the men sitting in irons, and sometimes they were delayed, or a case was held back, for practical or political reasons.

For John II and his mother, the regular estate business of the kind Richard handled had to be shunted into the background while they focused on finding a way to get John senior freed. It was essential to clarify what the allegations were, and to prove them groundless. It was essential to counter-attack, to lodge every possible complaint against the complainants (but carefully, carefully, for these were very powerful and influential men). It was essential to try to buy off enemies, and buy in friends. The Pastons were rich. This time more than any other, they had to use their assets.

The duke of Norfolk was core here. The dukes of Suffolk had never been friends of the Pastons, but Norfolk had been, not so long ago. Howard was at the front of the actions, but Norfolk stood behind him. Perhaps John senior had been unwilling to negotiate with Norfolk over Caister, but that stance had to be rethought now. The strategy meetings, the messages that ran between Hellesdon and the Inns of Court, must have focused most of all on what to offer Norfolk.

Did Richard have a hand in this? There is nothing to tell us. But he had acted as an intermediary with the duke before, and his brother was a vital contact in Framlingham. It seems from what followed (at least one letter passed between the Pastons and John Calle)[3] that perhaps the Calle brothers did do something to help. And young John II might have listened to Richard's advice regarding the duke a little more carefully than his father would have done.

Then suddenly the duke of Norfolk was no longer there to be offered anything. He had dropped dead. It was entirely unexpected. The duke had been a healthy man in his mid-forties.

It was inevitable that this would pull the actions up short, but even so, it is astonishing what a difference it made. Within a few days, John Paston had been released from jail – and not only that, he had the satisfaction of seeing John Howard take his place in the cells.[4] At about the same time the small troop of men who had held Caister for the duke of Norfolk withdrew, the monks let out their breath, the Pastons' servants moved back in, and all was as it had been a few months earlier, except that now the duke of Norfolk was a lad in his teens, no older or better seasoned than John Paston II.

Whatever deals were struck behind closed doors to cut the tangled knot at Framlingham, they did not extend to the rest of the Paston family crises. Cotton in Suffolk, for example, was not an estate that the duke of Norfolk particularly coveted. The duke of Suffolk might well have done, since he and his father had been christened there before his family sold the estate to Fastolf, but he too was not John Paston's adversary at Cotton. Thomas Fastolf had a part, and so did a powerful Norfolk lawyer and landowner called William Jenney – one of the dozen executors Fastolf had named in various draft wills – but the moving force seems to have been Judge Yelverton.

He and Jenney had picked on Cotton apparently at random. They made it clear that once they had it secure they meant to move on to another estate, and another, and another, till John Paston did not have a scrap of Fastolf's lands left.[5] It was not that Yelverton had a personal title to Cotton, or Jenney either: their aim was not to grab the land so much as to dispossess John Paston, and Thomas Fastolf's claim was their justification.

Church of St Mary, Martham, Norfolk

The first news came this time from a tenant of one of the large farms at Cotton, Edward Dale.[6] Dale was a well-connected man, not one to tolerate being shoved around. He seemed reasonably well disposed to the Pastons, and when Yelverton and his crew had come to demand rent in the name of young Fastolf, he had refused to pay. His stand had done him no good, though, because Yelverton and Jenney had come back shortly afterwards, rounded up thirty-six of his prime bullocks, and driven them off in lieu of payment. One of Dale's neighbours had encountered the drovers, and recognizing the beasts as Dale's, had challenged them. Yelverton had persuaded this man to give them a bond, effectively standing surety for Dale in return for the release of the cattle. And Dale in his turn had felt obliged to bail out the man by giving Yelverton his own bond, getting his cattle back by promising to pay the rent that was due by Michaelmas.

Dale could hardly have done anything else, or he would have landed his well-meaning neighbour in trouble, but his promise to pay gave substance to Thomas Fastolf's claim. Meanwhile Yelverton was working on winning round the estate's other tenants, and according to Dale he was succeeding. Fastolf had not been such a fine landlord, evidently, that the tenants had had no quarrels with him. Yelverton was promising to sort out a collection of old grievances, and they liked the idea.

Clearly it was high time the Pastons sorted out the grievances themselves, so they sent young John Pamping down to Suffolk. The next news came from Pamping in

Ipswich jail. Learning by chance where to find Yelverton and Jenney, he had gone to have words with them (in St Lawrence's Church), and Yelverton had accused him of breaching the peace and promptly had him arrested. He wrote cheerily enough: 'So I am with the jailer, with a clog on my heel ... wherefore please your mastership to send me your advice.'[7]

It needed more than advice. It needed a stronger Paston presence, to reassure tenants like Dale, hold a manor court and bang heads together, talk round the sheriff at Ipswich and get Pamping freed, and generally give Yelverton and Jenney cause to think twice. It needed Richard Calle, in short, and since John II was looking for a task, Richard enlisted him to help. This enabled him to argue that they needed a strong escort to keep the lad safe, so when they rode down to Cotton that October,[8] they took around a dozen men with them.

Cotton is an inland village, set in the fertile Suffolk farmlands not far from Bury St Edmunds, and more than a day's ride from Norwich. Richard and John II arrived there early on a Friday, so they must have stopped overnight on the way, staying at an inn perhaps, and going over the issues and their plans with the men they had brought with them.

The estate was blessed with a number of strong manor houses set in moats. Cotton Hall – from which those dukes of Suffolk had been taken for their christenings – must have been the biggest and best of them, a stone house with a leaded roof, set on the rising land above the village with its high-towered church.

Richard and John II probably went first to Dale, who told them that Yelverton's man Andrews, who had stayed on in the village, had said William Jenney would be returning to preside at the court. Richard and John's first task was to ensure they controlled any court that was held, so they sent word to Jenney (perhaps via this Andrews) that if he tried to convene one, they would resist him with force.

Andrews seems not to have been staying at Cotton Hall, so the Paston men next rode over to secure the place. By the time they had stabled their horses, dumped their packs and set a fire going, the news came that Jenney had got the message, and would not be coming to Cotton.

Less good news followed shortly afterwards, when a servant of the bishop of Norwich rode up to the hall and demanded to speak to John Paston. John II went out to talk to him, and learned that Jenney had retreated to the nearby estate of Hoxne, and complained about the threats to its owner, the bishop. Bishop Lyhert was willing to arbitrate, so would John Paston senior please ride to Hoxne and make his case?

Even if John senior had been in Cotton, this must have sounded like a bad idea. Plenty of the Pastons' enemies had been talking to the bishop, not to mention Jenney, who was at that moment sitting by his fire and planning to share his dinner. If they agreed to an arbitrator, it needed to be someone much more securely on their own side. So John II politely declined the bishop's kind offer.

The next thing was to send out summonses and hold their own court. Richard reported afterwards to John senior that the tenants were 'right well pleased' with the outcome, except for two named Thurburn and Agas. Well, no court can please everyone: if one man is found for, another is found against. John II had perhaps learned something of village politics and justice, and the Paston family had reinforced their claim to the estate.

It was going well, and it was a very good thing they had Dale on their side. But the farmers of Cotton were worried about what would happen next, and it was hard to blame them. The dozen men standing behind John II and Richard would not stay in the village long term, and as soon as they went, Yelverton and Jenney would send their own men back.

By the next day John II was restive. He announced that he thought the best thing was to take the quarrel into Jenney's back yard. The man had an estate not far from Cotton, so John planned to go there and distrain his cattle.

Realistically, that was not wise. Like getting John Howard to follow John Paston senior into jail, this tidy revenge would rebound on them. But John II was the young master, and Richard could not forbid him. Perhaps he did not even disagree with him: Richard too could be impetuous and stubborn on occasion. He settled for not going himself, and heard later that John II had found a herd of Jenney's cattle, removed exactly thirty-six of them, and driven them off into Norfolk.

While John II enjoyed this little enterprise, Richard set to the practical work of winning Cotton round. Andrews and his men had sworn that if the Paston men dared to stay more than two days they would be thrown out on their heels, so he settled for five days. While the other men backed him up in case of trouble, he walked about the place and talked to all the farmers and cottagers. He assured them the Pastons would make sure they were better off if they supported them than if they opposed them. (He added, when he wrote to John senior, that he hoped this was the case, and suggested that he might approach the archbishop of Canterbury for a letter confirming his support. That would kill the rumour that had reached Cotton, that the archbishop intended to determine Fastolf's will against John senior, and it would comfortably outweigh Jenney's bishop of Norwich.)

John senior, he knew, would want to know particularly about the rent, so he reported that he had extracted eight marks from the tenants who were overdue, and persuaded the rest to pay at Michaelmas. His master should take particular care with Dale, he added: the man should not be made to suffer from the obligation he had given to Yelverton.

Richard cannot have forgotten about poor John Pamping, though he probably had to leave other men to work on freeing him. Pamping was a resourceful lad, with lots of friends and relatives. He found some men to stand surety for him, and before too long he was out of Ipswich jail.

Church of St Mary the Virgin, Wilby, Norfolk

13
The bridge
over the
moat

Church of St Andrew, Cotton, Suffolk

Some children are born into families where going to jail is seen as a natural hazard of life: something regrettable, but not surprising. The Paston children were not of their number. True, criminals are found in the grandest of families as well as the meanest, but the Berrys, the Berneys, the Mautbys, were not people who expected to feel the cold chafe of iron on their wrists and ankles. These were respectable families, in which for generations men and women had kept well clear of illegal activity. The Pastons' background might be somewhat more obscure, but up till now the same had been true of that family. John Paston's grandfather, father, brothers: none of these, as far as we know, had visited a cell except as a lawyer advising the accused. And as well as being god-fearing, law-abiding people themselves, these families did not expect their servants to fall foul of the law.

When the news came that John Paston senior had been taken to jail, Margery's mother would have reassured her family, friends and servants that it was the result of a terrible misunderstanding. The family had enemies, they all knew that. John senior issued lawsuits against them, and not surprisingly they countered with lawsuits against him. But John Paston was of course in the right: he was the good man, his enemies at best deluded and at worst plain evil.

Then John Pamping had his spell in irons. Pamping seems to have been a likeable lad, literate and respectable: he might try to take his imprisonment gracefully, but that did not mean he took it lightly.

Two of their household in jail. Both were freed within days, and with no charges proved against them, but this must still have been seriously disconcerting.

When Richard Calle followed them into the cells, it would have been downright alarming.[1]

Of course it was not just alarming to young Margery, struggling to make sense of a world where the black and white certainties of her childhood had been mashed into mud. It was thoroughly alarming to Richard too. His family was also a respectable one whose members did not expect such things to happen. And he had not set out to break the law, only to do his job, as best he understood it. If he did not always agree with his master's actions, he clearly felt he had little option but to continue to serve that master loyally and obey his orders. And now doing that had driven him into a marsh.

Judge Yelverton was as quick as John Paston senior (or his father Judge Paston, back in his own day) to reach for a writ when things did not go his way, so it would have been no surprise that Richard and John II's efforts in Cotton had been followed back to Norfolk by a blizzard of legal paperwork. When the next tranche of trouble brewed at Cotton, Richard had known there was a warrant out for his arrest. To head down to Suffolk to try to resolve things would be to put himself in danger. However Pamping was in no better a position, was probably several years younger, and had shown himself at Ipswich to be less nimble at skipping out of reach of his enemies. So it was Richard who rode off to meet up with Edward Dale.

Dale had sent word that Yelverton and Jenney, in their claimed capacity as Fastolf's executors, had sold the Cotton estate, and the buyer and his son had moved to take possession. They had torn down the roof of Cotton Hall and melted the lead, and broken down the bridge over the moat.[2] Whatever the short-term joys of such vandalism, this was singularly short-sighted if they planned to live there. They had had to set a plank over the moat as a makeshift substitute, or they would not have been able to get into the house.

Then they sent to Dale with a demand for supplies. Dale refused to have any dealings with them, and received a mouthful of threats as a result. This was a point when he decided he could use Richard, John II and their twelve sturdy men. And if the twelve sturdy men had come with Richard, perhaps he could have thrown out the incomer and put things to rights. But they did not, and

Church of St Peter and St Paul, Bardwell, Suffolk

instead he was grabbed (apparently at Scole, on the Norfolk/Suffolk border) by Yelverton and Jenney's men. They acted on their warrant, and within hours Richard was listening to the charges against him being read by the sheriff.

He sent a message to John Paston senior, and waited for help. Paston himself had been freed very promptly when his family intervened, and Pamping too had not been left in jail long, so Richard could reason- ably assume that similar efforts would be made for him. Nothing happened. No sheriff's man came ambling down to his cell with the key and an announcement that now he was free to go. No letter came from John senior either.

This was worrying. Richard must have given it long enough for it to be clear that his master was not going to do anything, then he sent a message again, this time to his brother in Framlingham. He probably did so reluctantly. This was not his brother's problem, it was one that sat squarely at John Paston senior's door, and he should not have had to ask his brother to intervene. Also, he had no wish at this delicate time to ask for more favours from the duke of Norfolk.

John Calle must have thought much the same. But Richard was his blood, and in evident need of help, so he went up to the castle and got himself an interview with the new young duke. He must have put his case well – and the duke seems to have been a decent man – so Calle got what he asked for: a letter from the duke to William Jenney, ordering him to see Richard freed.

It should have worked, but it did not. Perhaps Jenney gambled that the new duke would not follow through if he ignored the request. Perhaps the duke, still a minor, genuinely did not have enough clout to knock Yelverton and Jenney's heads together. Quite likely Yelverton and Jenney put their own case to the duke (who must have been sorry that Caister, so much newer and more comfortable than draughty old Framlingham Castle, would not come to him after all), and managed to persuade him to change his allegiance.

Richard was left sitting in his cell. He was not as uncomfortable there as he might have been, or as isolated either, as his ability to send out messages makes clear. He had been chatting with the sheriff, discussing the situation and how it might develop. It would have been apparent to the sheriff that even if his friends had not yet seen Richard freed, he was not lying when he said he had plenty of them. Most of the Cotton tenants had come to visit him in jail, and probably a few other men too. It looked to the sheriff as if Richard would have no trouble persuading a Norfolk jury to acquit him of the charges. It was starting to look that way to Yelverton and Jenney as well. They decided the best way around this was to send Richard for trial at the King's Bench in London, but this presented problems of its own, not least in how best to transport Richard there. It was probably not something the sheriff had to do often, and he wanted neither to pay out a large sum for a secure escort, nor to see Richard escape and face a fine. Richard was offering sympathy while carefully fuelling his worries, with the result that nothing had been done, or looked likely to be done.

However, this was bringing him no nearer freedom, so he sent another letter. He must have thought over who best to write to, the obvious options being Margaret Paston, John II, or at a pinch William Paston (a much better lawyer, Richard probably reckoned, than his brother John senior, and a more reliable friend). He chose young John II, who knew all about Cotton and its problems, and a fair bit about the law as well. Judging by his letter, although Richard was making a good fist of the practical end of his situation, he was finding it harder to make sense of the legalities. John II might understand what the hillock of writs meant, how best to play the London and Norwich options against each other, and so on.

Perhaps with an eye to what John II would pass on to his father, he took care to emphasize that even in this somewhat inconvenient situation, he was not neglecting his duties as land agent. He was keeping up with the news from Cotton, thanks to his visitors, and giving thought to the money issues. The rents due at Michaelmas had inevitably been paid to Yelverton's men: they had made enough threats to give the tenants no other option. Richard had kept careful track of who had paid, a list that included 'all the great farmers'. He had learned that four men were installed in Cotton Hall, including 'one Manning, a tenant, a false knave',[3] plus one man's wife.

If he wanted most of all for John II to take action to see himself freed, Richard gave thought too to what the man could best do about Cotton. He seems to have trusted John II to take action, and he must have been angry enough that he was keen to see action taken. So it would be no bad thing for John II to ride to Cotton, he wrote, but he should not go to Dale's house, because Dale had had enough trouble already. He should head straight for the hall, equipped with ladders or planks so he would not be pulled up short at the moat, and enough men that he could overwhelm the residents. Then he should 'pull the knaves out by the head'.

He seems to have finished his letter later, because there was more news, and a different tone, in the last paragraphs.

First, the jail delivery that should have been held had been postponed, 'and all is done because of me'. Jenney had prevented the clerk from coming, for fear that Richard would be acquitted. He had been right to worry, Richard added, because 'I was through with the sheriff' and the jury had been 'made after my advice'. So he and the sheriff would have

been perfectly happy to see the delivery go ahead, and the sheriff was miffed that it had not been, because he had hoped to see eleven men leave the jail that day, and instead he was stuck with keeping them all. Anyway the postponement had been pointless, Richard added, because it seemed that the King's Bench writ that had been issued meant that even if he had been acquitted of felony locally, he could not have been freed himself.

Second, the sheriff had given him another piece of news. John Paston senior might not have replied direct to Richard, but he had done something. He had told the sheriff that he reckoned Richard was to blame for his own arrest.

That was mean and low of him. John senior had never been a brilliant master, but he had never before fallen so far short of what his servants could reasonably have expected of him. Richard must have felt bitter: how could he not be?

But not so bitter that he failed to think about how to respond. As well as being a hurtful and dangerous allegation, it was a thoroughly stupid one. The sheriff clearly did not believe it was true, which was hardly surprising, since Richard would have had to be little short of insane to arrange his own arrest. As he put it, 'there is no man so sore hurt as I am by the taking, both in loss and in also in reproof of my own person and of my friends'.[4] He tried to write moderately and politely (after all, the letter might well be seen by John senior), so he suggested that perhaps this was the result of his enemies whispering against him. And he emphasized that in spite of this blow, he was a faithful servant, and John senior 'hath my true service and shall have while that I live'.

This time, he got the reply he needed. With young John II playing his full part, the ruffians were thrown out of Cotton Hall, and the writs against Richard were thrown out too.

Richard met up with John Paston senior shortly after he was freed, possibly at the newly recovered Caister Castle. It must have been a difficult meeting. Obtuse as John could be at times, he surely realized he had acted unforgivably. But if Richard had hoped for an apology, it looks as if he did not get it.

There was nothing he could do but swallow his anger (though not forget), and get on with his job. A short while afterwards he wrote to report on his activities to John senior, as he was used to doing.[5] His letter suggests that he was working normally, and even making suggestions in the way he only did when he felt confident in his position.

He had been back to Cotton, as he had promised John II and the tenants, and made sure all was well after Yelverton's men had been thrown out. He had even collected some rent – £4 2s, less than Dale alone should have paid, but a creditable sum in difficult circumstances – and had expended it, as the Pastons had asked him to, on linen cloth for sheets, shirts and smocks. He had done some legal business in Nacton, and held a court in Calcott, another nearby Fastolf estate. He had negotiated with some truculent tenants at Mautby, and had not forgotten his instructions to pay the priests at Caister, which would be done as soon as he had enough money.

All this was well done, as he knew. He added that the price of malt had plummeted

in East Anglia, as had the price of corn, but he had heard that malt was selling well in Flanders, though he had not been able to confirm the price there. Since he knew of some merchants who were sending a ship over to Flanders, he had taken it upon himself to get them to carry over a hundred combs of malt. It might be even better, he added, to 'make some bargain with some of your beer brewers', but he did not like to do that without permission, which he was asking for in his letter.

There was news of the family – young Edmund, who was to go away to school after Christmas, and some messages for Clement. He must have been happy to be asked by Margaret to send these: it was a proof that she was firmly behind him. And he added a careful blessing at the end: 'My right reverent and worshipful master, Almighty Jesus preserve, further and keep you.' If it sounds overblown to us now, it probably did not do so to John Paston. Richard knew how to deal with his master.

And he perhaps had a hand too in the final piece in the mending of relations that took place that autumn. If it was in the interests of the Pastons to start off on a better footing with the new young duke of Norfolk, it was also in the interests of the Calle family to ensure that the good start that had been made was carefully built on. Young John III was now getting to an age when he needed something more substantial to do than running errands for his mother. He was given a place in the duke's household at Framlingham.

Church of St Mary the Virgin, Martham, Norfolk

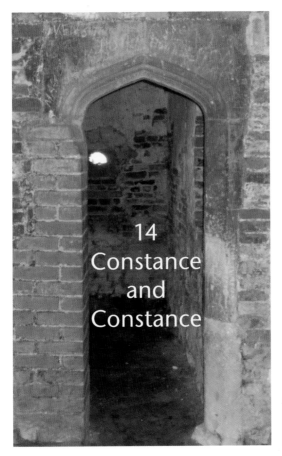

14
Constance
and
Constance

Caister Castle

Most quarrels are resolved after a while, even if that while is sometimes a long one, and by the middle of 1462 it must have seemed that the row about John II leaving court was well behind the Paston family. John II might have grumbled bitterly, but he had settled down to make himself useful in East Anglia, and there was little argument that he had indeed been useful. Richard Calle had taken pains to ensure that John was given credit for all he had done at Cotton, and what he had done at Cotton had ended with the Pastons regaining the estate, even though the hall was now little better than a wreck.

In the months that followed, though, relations between John II and his father did not settle down. Perhaps in part it was because John III was no longer there to act as a steadying influence on his big brother, and perhaps too it was because John II felt keenly the difference between his brother's situation and his own.

John III had a good position. Framlingham was a fair way from Westminster, socially as well as geographically, but the duke and duchess of Norfolk presided over a lively and cultured household, and John III was getting to know people with power and influence, and probably having an enjoyable time. John II might reasonably have felt that it should have been he, as the older brother and heir, who was jousting and hawking with the nobility. Certainly it would have been normal for him to obtain a position in another household at this point in his life, if he was not to work with his father and uncles at the Inns of Court. At least one of the Pastons' braver associates pointed out to John senior that people were talking in East Anglia about John II's lack of suitable employment.[1] He suggested (and perhaps enjoyed suggesting) that it was because John senior was so 'niggard cheap': positions such as John III's had to be paid for, and his father seemed averse to spending money on his heir.

Perhaps in part it was because, although this was a period of relative calm, the family's problems had not been resolved, and the stress of them continued to scrape away at the thin smooth surface of their lives. John senior had not relaxed, and he had no reason to relax. Yelverton, Jenney, Thomas Fastolf, the duke of Suffolk: none of them had resigned themselves to accepting his claims and making his life easy. Fastolf's old servants Howes and Worcester (Hanson had died that summer) were still not pacified, and still danger-ously open to being courted by those who did not accept John Paston's account of Sir John Fastolf's last days. The Pastons were spending more than they might on security, and taking in less than they might in rent; they probably still did not feel rich, and perhaps there were solid reasons why John II was not given the funds to make a showy appearance in a nobleman's household.

Perhaps too it was because John II, not a young man blessed with patience, found it hard to settle to the day to day tasks of estate management. Work of the kind that Richard handled did not seem to interest him at all: while his father's letters were full of the minutiae of crop sales and dealings with tenants, John II skipped airily above these prosaic details. He might have excelled at rustling William Jenney's cattle and attacking Cotton Hall, but these were not the skills that the family needed on the average Monday

in February. And in fairness, it would not have been normal for the heir to the family to be set to shadow its land agent: if John II cavilled at being pushed in this direction, he had some reason.

But perhaps it was none of these problems that brought things to a pitch where John II stormed out of the household. Off he went, claiming he would leave the whole lot behind – the writs, the grumbles, the thin-faced fear – and instead try to make his own way in life.

That did not end the arguments, it just changed their focus. Margery's father blamed her mother. He reckoned she had fixed this with her son, had agreed it was the best solution, but in fact she had not done so at all. Margaret Paston had not wanted this for her son; far from it. She had made real efforts to help John II achieve his ambitions, and she reckoned she had been 'right evilly paid' by him in return.[2]

For John II's father to grumble at him was normal, but for his mother to take this line was new and shocking. So what had John done?

Once again, the historical record is frustratingly silent on exactly what happened at this time. But

Church of St Andrew, Bedingham, Norfolk

there is one thing John II did at some point which must have caused a lot of upset to his family, so perhaps it was now that it occurred.

He fathered an illegitimate child.

There are many things that even the most riotously quarrelsome families do not talk about, so it is by no means certain that Margery knew this. Perhaps she knew only that John II had done something unforgivable. But quite likely she did know, because even in families where talk is forbidden, there are still whispers. Richard Calle almost certainly knew. Everyone in the Pastons' circle seemed to know that John II had grown into a cheerful womanizer. The lad should probably have been married, but his parents had made no noticeable move to arrange that for him, and in the absence of a wife he was taking his pleasure where he might. Visits from angry parents with a weeping daughter, rows behind closed doors, a son slamming the gate as he left: again, the details are lost to us, but the pattern is a familiar one from which any observant man might have drawn the right deductions, and Richard surely did.

The child – a girl – was given a mention in Margaret's will, years later, so it is clear the family did not abandon her or her mother.[3] (It was not a very generous mention – she was left ten marks – but then Margaret was not naturally a generous woman.) Her name was Constance. And some years later John II received a letter which he kept from a woman called Constance Reynforth,[4] so it is quite likely that this was her mother. There is no other mention in the family's papers of either Constance, so although they kept in contact, it was probably at a distance. When Constance wrote, it was not from Norfolk, but from Cobham in Surrey.

John II did not marry his Constance, so she was almost certainly not from an exalted family, which he and his parents would have been keen to ally with. But she was not a common prostitute either, or she would have been dropped without mercy. Perhaps she was a servant – even a servant of the Pastons themselves – or the daughter of an innkeeper or a craftsman, a girl he could not possibly marry for social reasons, but whose family was known to his own, and whom neither John II nor

Church of St Peter Hungate, Norwich

his parents were brutal enough to abandon. Perhaps she was the kind of girl, just a short distance socially below his own family, whom John II felt he could and should marry. If he suggested it, his parents gave him a very firm answer. It was the answer, to be fair, that most if not all people in their situation would have given: the family could not afford this, and it must not be done.

15
Three
hundred
marks
a year

All Saints Church, Edingthorpe, Norfolk

In November 1463 Margery Paston travelled up to Norwich from Caister with her mother.[1] Margaret wanted to buy some supplies: it was already cold, and was showing signs of becoming a particularly harsh winter. (Later that winter the rivers froze so hard that men could walk across the widest of them.) Margaret was often scathing about the quality of goods on sale in Norwich, and asked her husband and sons to buy garments in London instead, but this time she chose to do her shopping in the city.

What had once been a commonplace event must have been a small treat for the women at this time, when they were mostly cooped up at Hellesdon or Caister, and only ventured out of their gates when they could be sure of a good escort. They seem to have had a merry time roaming around the market and calling at the drapers' shops, picking out cloth and furs, ribbons and laces. When their errands were done they went to Elm Hill, to call on Grandma Paston.[2]

Agnes Paston in a bad mood could probably have quelled their merriness in a second, but this time they were in luck: she had company already, so there would be no lectures. And there emerged a chance to meet someone new, since among the visitors who arrived subsequently was a man called Wrothe, whom Margery and her mother seem not to have known beforehand.[3] He turned out to be a relative of Elizabeth Clere, the friend (and relation) who had worried about Elizabeth Paston's treatment some years earlier.

Master Wrothe was complimentary about Margery. 'A goodly young woman', he called her.

To that Agnes replied that she was a goodly young woman who needed a husband, and if Master Wrothe knew of any man who might do, her family would be glad to hear of it.

Margery might well have cringed at that. But it was true, she was getting to the age

Church of St Mary the Virgin, Martham, Norfolk

when her parents ought to be seeking out a husband for her. So she would have listened with interest when Master Wrothe replied that he did know of a man he thought might prove suitable. This was the son of Sir John Cley, who was chamberlain to the dowager duchess of York. As Margaret Paston probably took the opportunity to point out, a couple of years previously the duchess had stayed with her daughters in the Southwark house that they had had from Sir John Fastolf, and her son who was now King Edward had visited them there every day.

Margaret herself had not visited the Southwark house at that time, so she had probably not the benefit of Sir John Cley's acquaintance (or of the king's either). So it was news to her, as well as to Margery, that he had a son of eighteen, and very interesting news that when he came of age the son would inherit lands worth 300 marks a year.

When the other visitors were gone, the Paston ladies had a chance to discuss this information more frankly. Agnes reckoned it was a time when marriages could be got pretty cheap, with the world so uncertain. Margery might get a man with a decent income, like this Cley boy, without having to be given a large dowry. Three hundred marks was not a vast fortune, but it was a sum that would enable her to live the kind of life the Pastons had been used to before the Fastolf inheritance. Sir John Cley was no lord, but he was a respectable man who knew and was known by the king. So this was definitely an opening worth pursuing.

There is no indication that Margery's own opinion was asked. There is nothing particularly pleasant about being treated as a burden to be disposed of as cheaply as possible, but Master Wrothe's compliments must have put her in a good mood, and she probably agreed on the whole with her mother and grandmother. She was still very young – thirteen or fourteen, perhaps – and had had no time to become disillusioned with the hard-edged business of bargaining a marriage. This did not sound like the grandest of matches, but her mother and grandmother seemed to think it a promising opening, and there were advantages for a girl in marrying early. There would be advantages, come to that, in removing herself from all her family's miseries: the endless watching-out for enemies, the tales of prison cells and all the rest of it. Change her name, gain her own household to run: there was plenty to like in that prospect. She had not met young Master Cley as yet, so she could hardly have a personal opinion of him, but eighteen and solvent was a good beginning. Many women fared worse.

So Margery might well have been hopeful, gone back to Caister and confided to Anne that there was a plan to marry her off.

But it was not actually a plan, it was only a mention. Margaret Paston did get John Daubeney to write down an account of these conversations, and send it off to her husband. But John Paston senior had plenty of things to occupy him, and so did Margaret herself. They probably both reckoned there was no urgency. Neither John II or John III had married yet. Perhaps it was a time when marriages could be got cheap, but it was also one when the Pastons continued to be in a precarious position. In a year or two the lawsuits would surely be concluded, they would be happily confirmed in possession of all the Fastolf lands, and then perhaps they could be more ambitious for Margery.

As far as we can tell, Margery heard no more.

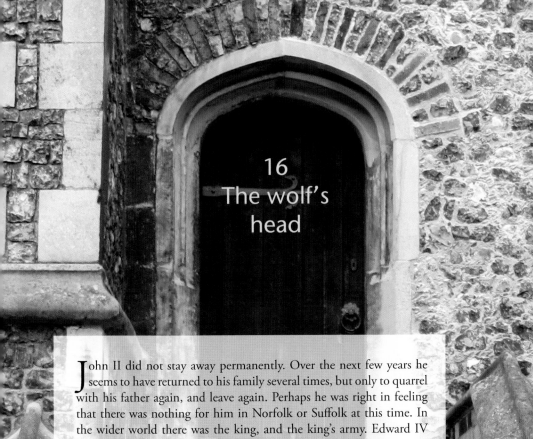

16
The wolf's head

John II did not stay away permanently. Over the next few years he seems to have returned to his family several times, but only to quarrel with his father again, and leave again. Perhaps he was right in feeling that there was nothing for him in Norfolk or Suffolk at this time. In the wider world there was the king, and the king's army. Edward IV had singularly failed to bring in the secure government that so many had hoped for, and was facing renewed threats from Henry VI's queen, acting on behalf of her young son. The younger Pastons had by now put themselves firmly in the Yorkist camp, and they continued to support Edward throughout the troubles of these years. John senior stayed distant from the political wrangles and the pitched battles, but John II played some part in the king's forces (it is difficult to tell how much of one), and John III did too, serving in the north under the duke of Norfolk.

This brought them new friends, and freed them from their father's dark shadow. What he had not achieved through the usher of the king's chamber, John II was achieving now: he was getting to know the king.

Meanwhile the middle 1460s must have dragged for those Pastons who stayed at home. How long could it take to determine a will? When men on all sides were filing new lawsuits at regular intervals, and when the government was churning, and there was no continuity in hearings and decisions, the answer clearly was, years and years. And years.

How often could a man spend time in prison, before his good reputation was lost forever? That is perhaps less easy to say, but as John Paston found himself returning to the Fleet again and again, the dirt of the dungeons stuck to him more and more indelibly.

A man in the Fleet who could muster some money (even if he had to borrow it from his brothers, or leave his servants unpaid) could buy both comforts, and the ability to carry on his affairs. John Pamping continued to serve John senior when he was a prisoner, and to convey letters and messages from him to his wife, and from Caister and Hellesdon to London. John's brothers William and Clement probably called on him too, to discuss tactics and take instructions, and so did other of his servants from time to time.

But this was not an easy way to do business. And when John senior was not in prison, he was watching out all the time for fear he would be apprehended by a sheriff's clerk with a writ and escorted there. There were worse threats too to be wary of, in particular that he might fail once more to attend a hearing he had been summonsed to appear at, and be declared an outlaw as a result. This was one of the strongest penalties the English legal system had to offer, since it removed all legal protection for a man. In the eyes of the law, his was a wolf's head: he could be treated like a wild animal and killed on sight. (His goods were all forfeit as well, a serious problem for his family, if hardly relevant to the dead man himself.)

The Pastons' enemies had made many threats over the years to kill John senior. If they managed to get him outlawed, it would give them the right to do so.

Nor was John senior the only one dodging writs. One advantage for John II in staying away from East Anglia was that he was less likely to be apprehended by a group of men waving summonses and handcuffs. The Paston estate servants were facing charges too. Richard Calle and John Daubeney, and another of their colleagues, Thomas Bond, must have been particularly worried by the judgement that was given against them in 1465,[1] since it not only gave their accusers the right to arrest them, it specified that they would then not be freed from prison unless they paid a surety of 800 marks. This was probably considerably more than any of them possessed. They could not have been confident that if they did land up in jail, their master would find the money to bail them out. So month after month, when they rode round the Paston lands to collect rents and negotiate over crops, they had to take great care where they went and who they spoke to, and to rely on friendly men to warn them if any of their enemies had been seen in the area.

The first time John senior's enemies called for a determination of outlawry was late in 1464. William Jenney got two judgements for damages against him in the Suffolk courts, and fixed a hearing that he did not attend. He was saved by King Edward. Perhaps John II had a part to play here: he might have both learned what was proposed, and had a chance to argue to the king against it. The king decided not to grant the appeal, but to make further enquiries. He announced that he did not wish to see a man outlawed for 'so little substance',[2] and wanted to check whether Paston had issued writs in response to those Jenney had laid down.

It would have suited Jenney very well to call a hearing that John senior could not learn about until it was too late, but it cannot have been so very easy to do so, especially when there was a bundle of Paston brothers monitoring activity in the courts. And there is no proof that it was underhand dealing that caught John senior out repeatedly, while there is some reason to believe that it was at least as much his own failings. Stress, muddle, confusion, a failure to prioritize: probably all of these played a part. Richard Calle, Margaret Paston, and others too had been reminding John senior for years of things he needed to do – counter Thomas Fastolf's 'evidences', write to John Calle after he had intervened with the duke, pay off William Worcester, and plenty more on the same lines. As far as can be told, he regularly failed to do what was necessary.

So essential though it was that he respond immediately to the king, and make a good case against Jenney and his other accusers, it is conceivable that he did not. Whatever he did, or did not do, Jenney's next attempt was successful. On 20 November the king issued a proclamation that John Paston senior was now an outlaw, and his goods should be forfeit.[3]

This landed him back in the Fleet, which was not entirely a disaster: no one could kill him while he was within the prison walls. And it focused not just his mind, but those of his brothers, his servants and associates. Many candles must have been burned, reams of paper expended in drafts of counter-claims, and likely as not a fair bit of money disbursed in useful quarters. It worked, for a while at least. He was discharged from his outlawry and freed from the prison. But by June 1465 he was back in the Fleet, and this time it seems that he stayed there for at least six months.

It is hardly surprising that no more was heard of possible marriages for Margery, or for her brothers and sisters, over these months. Many people's affairs were sitting stagnant while the Yorkists and Lancastrians battled for the throne, and a father in jail added a further reason to do nothing but wait for better days.

Nor do we know much else about Margery during this time. She might possibly have been boarded for a while with another family, much as had been done for her aunt Elizabeth and her brother John III (and was common among families of their station), but there is no evidence of it. And even if her parents had tried to find her a position, it might have proved difficult: those who supported the Pastons in private might have hesitated to make their allegiance public when they had so many powerful enemies.

So more likely she spent her time at home with her mother. Wars provide their share of dull routine, and Margery would have carried on going to church, visiting the tenants, sewing sheets and shirts. She probably took a part in minding the younger children and teaching them their letters, and caring for them when they were sick. But she would not have been permitted to do anything that could be seen as servants' work, and Margaret Paston was a woman who kept her own firm hand on the household's management. So the scope for her daughter was limited, and it would have been unsurprising if sometimes – especially when the family was facing a crisis, not making social visits, and the children were kept close to home – she was jagged with boredom.

One other possibility is perhaps worth considering.

all images: Church of St Mary Magdalene, Mulbarton, Norfolk

If most of the law is embodied in possession, the other portion of it is evidence. In every case when the Pastons had faced challenges, their friends had advised them to waste no time in producing their evidence. Deeds of land transfer, tax records, court rolls: the kind of evidence that could be useful depended on the context, but there was no context in which evidence did not play its part. As well as the need for documents to prove possession of estates, there was a need for documents to prove lineage: an increasingly pressing issue for the Pastons, because their enemies were trying to build up the old argument that they came from servile stock.

A problem with evidence is of course that it does not always exist, or if it does exist, it is not easily findable. But one useful feature of written evidence is that when necessary, what might tactfully be called 'creative research' can be used to produce it.

The Pastons were sure this had been used against them. Margaret Paston had made scathing comments about documents on which the wax seals were not yet cold after the fiasco at Gresham.[4] Now, under the heavy shadow of the Fleet, they needed to quash any scruples they might have felt, and ensure it was used for them as well.

This had to be done clandestinely, and by those either within the family, or very closely tied to it. Even their long-established associates were not easily trusted, in a region where enemies as well as friends worked with each other and married into each other's families. Margery's parents were fully occupied with the public side of the family's affairs: running the household and the estates, dealing with the servants, pursuing cases at law (and negotiating with prison warders). So were her uncles William and Clement. John II and John III had their own activities, and were often not at home. Who was left? The women.

There were two women in the family who might have had the leisure (and the education, the ability, the sharp wits) to play a hand in this. One was Elizabeth. She had not as yet remarried, and although her brothers had helped her fight back against her husband's relatives after his death, and probably recover at least some of his lands (in later life she

did not just recover from this low point, she became very rich[5]), she would not have been running a large household of her own at this time. She was probably living mostly in London, in lodgings like her brothers. Elizabeth seems never to have been close to John senior, but she was close to her other brothers, William and Clement, and just as they chose to overlook their differences with John to help him secure the Fastolf estate, perhaps their sister was persuaded to do so, and to give practical help in return for her brothers' help to her.

There are only a few mentions of Elizabeth in the Pastons' surviving papers, but one from John II is intriguing: it mentions getting from her 'an answer of such matters as she wotteth [knows] of'.[6] Why write so cryptically, in a private letter? The obvious reason is that the issue they had to discuss was one so sensitive that they dared not risk a mention falling into the wrong hands.

Margery was no longer a child, and she too had time to spare, few public obligations and a degree of education. Writing formal documents was not the easiest of tasks, in an period when the writers needed to mix their own ink and sharpen their own quills, but plenty of people managed it, not all of them men. Elizabeth and her niece would not have known enough of the law and its conventions to be confident in drafting and writing out deeds and court judgements unaided, but there were other members of the family who could have guided them, showing them samples perhaps, and telling them to make a copy while changing a name here and there. They could have learned to age parchment and finish off the documents with battered seals and dingy ribbons. Existing documents were perhaps adapted, with smudges, crossings-out and a hole or two torn in convenient places to ensure the meaning was the one required, as well as new ones being produced.

Whoever did this work, clearly it was done.[7] At some point, probably in late 1465 or early 1466, the family delivered a solid stack of documents to the king's officers. They included 'diverse great evidences and court rolls' which were designed to show how the

Church of St Margaret, Paston, Norfolk

family had a long history in Paston village (or as it was described, 'the town of Paston'). Far from being bondmen, so these papers showed, they had possessed bondmen of their own. They had held courts in the village, as only the lord of the manor was entitled to do. There were papers about court fees, taxes, inquests, proving that they had played the part of a gentry family from time out of mind – or at least, going comfortably back to King Edward I.

There was proof that the Pastons had maintained their own chaplain, of their patronage of religious houses. Deeds dated and undated detailed landholdings and contracts of marriage with other gentry families. Some hinted (but here they would have needed to be even more cautious) that the Pastons shared the blood of some of the most worshipful and exalted families in the land.

As a final touch, the family set about proving their descent from Norman knights who had come over to England with the Conqueror. The first known ancestor was one Wulstan, a kinsman of Sir William Glanville; his son was another Wulstan, and his sons were Ralf and Robert, and Robert's sons were Edmund and Walter, and so on down to the present day. John senior had done some research into the duke of Suffolk's family, which – as was well known and often mentioned – was not nearly as grand as might have been expected, and could reliably be traced back to Yorkshire ferry keepers and fishermen.[8] It must have given him a certain satisfaction to put together a lineage that was better than the noble duke's.

As well as the work on the document themselves, a degree of research was needed on the ground. Documents could not be 'discovered' in Paston unless someone had been in Paston and made a show of searching for them. Indeed there was a good argument for doing much, if not all, of the work up at Paston. It was by the bleak north Norfolk coast, on the road to nowhere. The Pastons – Margery's grandmother especially – had picked enough quarrels with its cottagers over the years, taken enough pains to separate themselves socially from them, that there can have been few callers at Paston Hall. Where better to settle down in a well-lit corner, and pen the words that would make the family secure?

Even if the truth is a little different, the effort involved was large enough – as was the eventual impact, when this cartload of evidence was delivered – that the family's adult members must all have had a good idea of what was being done. Did Richard Calle also know, or even help with the activity? We cannot know for sure, but it seems more likely than not. Whoever planned the campaign (John senior, or conceivably John II, or William or Clement) would have needed to entrust one or two servants with the secret, if only so they could carry messages between Norwich or Hellesdon and Paston. Apart from Father Gloys (and perhaps he too took a hand), no member of their team was better established in the family's service or more familiar with its affairs than Richard. And a man who regularly worked with the Pastons' papers, as Richard did, and who had himself urged John senior to find more and better evidence of his claims, could hardly have failed to appraise the situation when that evidence was eventually produced.

Richard knew about some of the lengths the Pastons had previously gone to, and he and his brother might have been closely involved with the efforts to win round the duke of Norfolk. The Pastons were never such fools as to make detailed notes of their bribes and under the table deals, but common sense says that whoever sat down with the duke to discuss the Caister situation offered him more than a bended knee and a nicely worded plea. When John Calle wrote to John senior afterwards, it would not have been about his brother's welfare; it must have touched on the part he had played in the negotiations, and perhaps on a promised reward he had not yet received.

Richard had been at pains since then to assure John senior of his loyalty, even – especially – at times when it had been severely strained. Perhaps this too is a kind of evidence that he was implicated in all that was being done behind closed doors, tied tight to the Pastons, and they to him, because of everything that he knew.

Walcott, North-east Norfolk

17
The drones,
the bees

'You may verily understand that [the work on my estates] is not guided wittily or discreetly, and therefore I pray you heartily to put all your wits together and see for the reformation of it.'[1] So John Paston senior wrote to his wife and his servants John Daubeney and Richard Calle, in a very long letter, full (like most of his letters) of instructions and demands, in January 1465.

It is never pleasant to receive criticism, and it is no less unpleasant when it is unjustified. Whatever John Paston imagined, he was not merely moderately well served by his wife and his estate managers, he was astonishingly well served by them. There is nothing, in the stacks of letters sent and received by the Pastons and their household, to suggest that Margaret and her team slacked when her husband was in London. And the servants who had weathered threats, fights and spells of imprisonment in the course of their work, and still carried on loyally in the Pastons' service, could have used gratitude and encouragement, not this mean-minded tirade.

But if Richard resented the tone of his master's letter – on Margaret's and his friend and colleague Daube's behalf as well as his own – he probably appreciated some of the reasons behind its writing. As John senior pointed out in the same letter, he was desperately short of money. The priests and poor men at Caister had not been paid their stipends, many of his servants were also behind with their wages, and John senior had received nothing from the estate towards his own expenses in London for a good year. This was an alarming contrast with the days before he had taken on the Fastolf estates, when in spite of problems like the Gresham affair, he and Margaret had normally been able to tuck away a handy sum in their coffers each year. For the previous few years they had been dipping into those reserves, and now, it seems, they were all but exhausted. The income from the Fastolf lands should have more than covered the expenses they gave rise to, including the college of priests, 'though part thereof be in trouble', as even John senior had to admit. But it was not coming close to doing so.

Perhaps he did not realize how much trouble there was, and how difficult it would be to increase the revenue from the estate. But pointing that out to him would solve nothing. Things had to change, and working harder was not going to bring about that change.

By this time Margaret had clearly concluded how they should change, because in the same letter John replied to a suggestion she had made. Perhaps it was one that she had talked over with Richard; even if it was not, it was probably one that he saw the sense in. She wanted John II (or Sir John, as people now called him, since he had been knighted by the king when he came of age) to come home.

This would be no easy solution. Margaret clearly knew that as well as her estate servants did, and she did not hide from them her awareness of it. Not only did she need to win John senior round to the idea, she had to persuade Sir John to return. There is no indication that he was eager to do so: she had to convince him it was necessary, even if his father stayed well back from the case she made.

And second, if Sir John did condescend to spend a while in Norfolk, they all needed to ensure that he proved an asset and not a drain on their resources. Had the years with the king and his army driven some sense into the lad? They would only find out by working with him. If he did any work, that is: for as his father put it, 'I could never feel or understand him to be sensible nor diligent in helping himself, but only as a drone among bees, which labour to get honey in the fields while the drone does nothing but take his part of it.'[2]

Margaret was also clearly as worried as his father that Sir John would prove a bad influence on the other young men in the household. She had taken to lecturing John III both in her letters and during their occasional meetings about the need to resist temptation,[3] and if she could not quite lecture Calle and Daubeney in the same vein, she might well have wished she could.

So this was not a foolproof way of solving all the family's problems, but it was

Church of St Margaret, Stratton Strawless, Norfolk

probably the least bad option. There needed to be a male Paston prominently visible in East Anglia, especially when John senior was kept in London by the weight of paperwork or the walls of a cell, and it needed to be the heir, to send the message to their enemies that the family was strong and united. And if that male Paston supervised some of the estate staff, it would free Richard and the rest of the team to spend more time trying to bring in money.

This was an argument John senior accepted, and by that May it was agreed how it would be done – or at least, tried. Sir John would come to Caister, to meet with his mother: not his father, not yet, and perhaps not ever. There had been rumblings at Hellesdon, where the tenants had seen all too much of Master Philip, the land agent working for the rival claimant to the estate, the duke of Suffolk, so Margaret wanted to be there as much as she could. If all went well, she would be able to leave Sir John at Caister to supervise that household, and perhaps absorb the good influence of the priests.

John Daubeney travelled down from Hellesdon to Caister with Margaret, and he travelled back up there with her a day or two afterwards, so Richard probably heard how it had gone from him. It sounded as if Sir John was hardly chastened and reformed, and as if he and Daubeney, 'a lewd fellow', as Margaret called him,[4] had brought out the worst in each other, which explained why Daubeney had been removed so promptly from his side. Still, it had been agreed that Sir John would run things at Caister for a while at least, and meanwhile Daubeney and another three men were to ride round the tenants at Hellesdon and Drayton, and make sure the spring ploughing started off well.

Perhaps it started well, but it did not continue well. Richard must have hoped that this would give him a chance to visit some of the more far-flung estates. But the kind of trouble that scampered out of the Hellesdon burrows did not need Daubeney's ham-handed methods, it called for his own best skills. So when he was brought news of it he cancelled whatever plans he had made, and rode out to Hellesdon.

The stretch of road between Norwich and Hellesdon was normally a busy one, not the sort of isolated track where a traveller needed to fear highwaymen lurking in the woods, but there was no safe road in East Anglia for a man who wore Paston livery at this time, so Richard would not have travelled alone. He would have joined another party, or taken a man or two with him.

It would have been a pleasant ride along the Wensum, between the scrubby chalkland used for rabbit warrens and the damp expanse of the water meadows, up to and past the watermills with their churning wheels. This was the lambing season, the time for the cows to be turned out to graze on the spring grass, the cottagers to be planting their crops; a time of year when there would normally have been a good scattering of people on the fields as well as the road. But when he got onto the Hellesdon estate the fields would have been unseasonably empty. The farmers were keeping their animals close in their barns, and sitting by them with staves and axes.[5] They knew all about the exchanges with the duke of Suffolk's men, and they reckoned the trouble was far from over.

Richard probably headed first to Hellesdon Hall. Daubeney, or his messenger, would have told him the gist of the story before he set off, but before he took any action he needed to learn of any new developments, and not least to find out whether Suffolk's men

were still around, and if so, where. Anyway, Daubeney's idea of what had to be done might not be Margaret Paston's, and it would be her instructions he had to follow.

The main building at Hellesdon was of stone, and stronger than the old manor at Gresham, but it was less strong than Caister Castle. It was not impregnable, and they could not realistically make it so. But the servants would have done what they could to secure it, so Richard would have been greeted by closed gates, shuttered windows, men peering through narrow slits to discover who had come before they opened up and let him in.

And by relief that he was come. Margery and her sister were probably at the house with their mother. The family and servants would all have come to welcome him in the yard, before Margaret dispersed them, a groom took his horse to be rubbed down, and he followed Margaret into the solar, or perhaps the chantry, the room (judging by the name, perhaps originally a chapel, or a place still sometimes used as one) that he used when he worked out of Hellesdon. There they would have gone over the events of the previous days, and planned what they could best do now.

It had started when a man named Piers Warren, though men knew him better as lazy Piers, had joined the rest of the Drayton and Hellesdon farmers in taking out his ploughing team. This Piers was not one of the Paston tenants, he was Suffolk's man, and he had been ordered over to Drayton by Master Philip. When Daubeney and the rest had found him ploughing a Paston field, they had told him to get off it sharpish. A 'flickering fellow', as Margaret called him,[6] lazy Piers was not a man to look for trouble, but he was more scared of Master Philip than he was of the Paston men, and he protested that he dared not disobey his orders. So Daubeney and his mates had stopped him by confiscating the mares that were pulling the plough.

That was Daubeney's style, as it had been Sir John's back at Cotton, but a distraint like that was bound to bring retaliation, and of course it had. Eighty men had ridden over from the duke's estate at Costessey. The Paston men had carried off two mares, so the Suffolk men had orders to find four horses that they could distrain. They did not bother to look for Piers Warren's mares, they took the first four they came across: two from a tenant called Stermyn, and two that belonged to the parson. (The parson had some land to farm, and he had a man and two horses to plough it for him.)

The parson was an old man, but Stermyn was younger, and angry enough to act first and think second. He had gone to Costessey to protest. Master Philip had met with him, and told him that the horses would not be returned until Warren's horses were given back. He had added for good measure that if the Pastons' men distrained so much as a hen in future, his own men would grab an ox in return, and if they couldn't find beasts in the fields to satisfy them, they would break into the tenants' houses and grab their goods.

Probably true, Richard must have reckoned, and Margaret too. Eighty men sent a powerful message. Indeed, the message they sent was not just that the duke's men would retaliate, it was that they were planning to go further on the offensive. Piers might have been pushed out of the gate first, but he was not the only man in the duke's livery who would be sent to steer his plough across the fields of Drayton and Hellesdon.

Even if the Pastons had mustered eighty men themselves (and there was no money to pay for that scale of protection, as Richard well knew), the duke could easily have upped

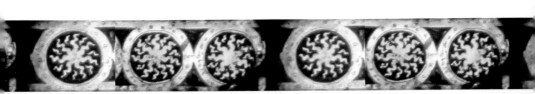

his forces to twice that many, or four times, or more. They could not win a war of attrition. Realistically all they could do was to reassure the parson and the tenants, find out Master Philip's surname so they could put it on the writs,[7] and try to ensure the cases went before a judge who would look on their complaints with sympathy.

That was Richard's job, or rather the start of it was. Margaret and her lawyer relations would have to carry it onwards.

A word or two of reassurance to Margaret, that he would do the best he could. A smile for the girls perhaps, a bit of banter with the brewer and the groom. Then back on his horse, and up to the church with its little bell tower.

He tracked down the parson, but he must have realized as soon as she saw the man that it was useless looking to him to play any further part in this. If Piers Warren was a flickering candle, the parson was so ancient and feeble he was close to being blown out. Margaret had wanted him to file a suit, complain to the courts that his horses had been stolen, but he flatly refused. As he pointed out to Richard, no judge in Norfolk could be trusted to find against the duke. So taking action against him would not get his horses back, and it would mark the parson out as a target for further punishment.

Richard was not going to force him. Fair enough, he said, and rode on to Stermyn's farm. He did no better there. Stermyn reminded him that he did not have to guess at the threats that would be made if he took any more action: he had already heard them to his face.

So Richard returned to the manor and told all this to Margaret. He probably guessed from her reaction that she would wait till he had left, then ride round to talk to the men herself. Did John Paston really expect this of her? The wonder of it was, whether he expected it or not, he was getting it from her. Margaret probably never told anyone what she really thought about the Fastolf inheritance. She just worked loyally to do what her husband wanted her to do: everything humanly possible, and then some more.

For himself, he seems to have fixed on his limits. He would do a thorough job; he was willing to face a bit of danger. (In fact it was more than a bit, it was a great deal of danger, and he knew it.[8]) But this was not a cause that a man should die for. He would not ask that of himself, or of the parson, or of Daube. As for the Pastons, he did not ask anything of them, or waste his breath advising them. He might have felt sorry for young Margery and her little brothers and sister, though. Barricaded into the house while their mother worked herself into a skeleton, and their father blundered into prison cell after prison cell: what kind of life was that for them?

There was nothing more he could do at Hellesdon. And there was plenty of other work waiting for him.

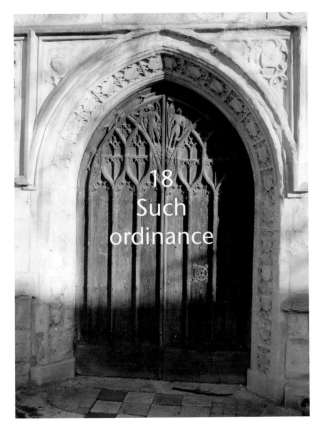

18
Such
ordinance

Church of St Miles Coslany, Norwich

Margery seems to have been at Hellesdon for much of the time in the summer of 1465, although as usual the mentions of her in the Pastons' letters are sparse, so it is impossible to know exactly when she was there, and when in Norwich, Paston or Caister. But she probably stayed mostly at her mother's side,[1] so it is most likely that she was at the manor when Margaret first sent Richard Calle to talk to Stermyn and the parson, then after Richard had ridden off, set out to talk to them herself.

This achieved no more than Richard had. And it was probably apparent to all of the family that whether the Pastons fanned the flames with a new batch of writs, or sat quiet and waited, would make little difference. At some point, and soon, the duke of Suffolk's men would make a serious attempt to seize the Hellesdon and Drayton estates.

If they did so, the Pastons had to resist it. What Margaret did next was to send to Sir John at Caister, to get together as many men as he could, arm them as well as possible, and bring them to Hellesdon. Perhaps she sent Margery and the younger children away at this point, but perhaps she did not. Norwich would have been little safer, and if they went anywhere else servants would have had to go with them, which would have reduced the number of men at Hellesdon.

So probably Margery was still there for her brother's arrival, at the head of his troop of soldiers. Sir John in his armour must have seemed very different from the bored and restless brother who had moped around Hellesdon a few years earlier, strewing books, friends and hawking equipment across the hall. He was a knight now, and knew how to

act like one: not just to tilt his lance in the jousting ground, but how to handle a crossbow and gun in earnest. His mother could stand aside now, he made clear: no need for her to act as the 'captainess'[2] when she had a grown son determined to defend his own inheritance. Margery and Margaret probably did not know whether to be more relieved or disconcerted.

Sir John had brought perhaps forty or fifty men with him, armed with crossbows and longbows, pikes and lances, and guns. There were not this many men capable of fighting on the staff at Caister, so he must have recruited some in Yarmouth, Norwich or other places nearby. Many of these soldiers for hire would have had their own weapons and armour, and for the estate servants and others with a strong right arm but nothing much else beyond a stave, Sir John would have raided the stores at Caister. So it was a motley group, probably wearing a basic version of the Paston livery – a coloured rag round their arm would be enough to mark them out – and sporting everything from the latest ordinance to rusty breastplates and halberds that might well have been used at Agincourt fifty years earlier. John Daubeney and the other local estate servants joined them, and some of the time Richard Calle was there too, so in all, the Pastons had about sixty men to defend their lands.

These men had all to be fed and housed, although that was easier in July than it would have been in a snowy winter. The stables, the brewhouse, the sheds: every building within the yard fence filled with packs and weapons. Some of the newcomers probably joined the cooks in the manor kitchen, and the aroma of sheep and rabbit roasting and bread baking drifted over the yard. The barrels in the brewhouse would soon have emptied, with the brewer working frantically to make new stocks of ale. Sir John also commandeered the church; the men stacked their sheaves of arrows, their guns, their padded jackets and steel armour in the steeple, and dossed down in the nave. The old parson, if he was wise, found a friend to stay with well away from Hellesdon.

The manor house itself was probably already as secure as it could reasonably be made, but more could be done, had to be done, to protect the tenants and their livestock. Some of the men rounded up the flocks of sheep that grazed on the water meadows and drove them off to Cawston, well to the north, where they were put to graze temporarily on the heath.[3] Cattle, pigs, hens, and strongboxes too: everyone at Hellesdon must have been desperate to move their goods to somewhere safer.

It was done just in time. On a Monday afternoon in that July of 1465, the duke's men arrived.

There were three hundred of them, a big enough force that those at the manor would have seen them coming from a good way off. Any men working within a mile or so of the house must have scrambled back inside the fence, and they had time enough to latch and bar the gates, shutter the windows, pull on their jackets and grab their weapons, though probably not to retrieve the gear they had left in the church. Any man with an indictment on his head – Richard was one, though perhaps he was not at the manor when this happened – kept well out of sight. The woman servants and the children would also have retreated into the house, so they probably saw little or nothing of what happened next, and had to wait for the men to tell them afterwards.

Inside the house, it must have been frustrating. At best they could glimpse a little movement through the cracks in the shutters, hear an indistinct shout or two. They had a long wait. They would not have had weapons like the soldiers, but they had probably grabbed whatever was at hand so they could defend themselves if it came to the worst: a stick, a scythe, a solid steel pan.

At last came the sound of the men marching off; and even then, Margaret probably made them keep inside the house till they heard their own men knocking on the door. It's safe now! In the yard, the men would have been taking off their helmets, stacking their bows back under cover, wiping the sweat from their brows.

So they did not attack?

And claimed they had never intended to, although no one at Hellesdon Hall would have believed that. It did not require three hundred men to deliver a peaceable message.

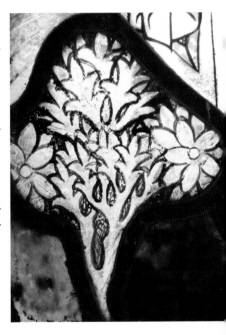

The men – headed by Master Philip and the bailiff of Costessey, the duke himself had not come – had demanded two things, Sir John said. First, they wanted to negotiate over the manor, and second, they wanted handed over to them those of the Pastons' men with warrants out for their arrest. They had sent for a couple of the bishop of Norwich's men to act as intermediaries, and the reason for the long delay was that both sides had waited for these men to arrive.

Not that he was prepared to negotiate, Sir John added. He would have offered nothing, handed over no one, if one of his men – one Naunton, who was perhaps one of the regular estate workers – had not offered to act as a hostage to break the deadlock. There was no warrant out for Naunton, so he was not risking jail – or not immediately – and should be freed once the one agreement that had been made was fulfilled: that both the duke's men and the Paston forces would leave the Drayton and Hellesdon estates.

Sir John had refused the offer of mediation, and the suggestion by one of the duke's men, Master Harleston, that it would be best if he came to meet with the duke himself. Harleston had made out it was all but his duty, since the duke of Suffolk was the lord of these parts. But the Pastons were not convinced that Suffolk was their good lord, or that Bishop Lyhert's men could be relied on to judge the issues neutrally.

If Richard was not at Hellesdon when this happened, he probably first got a sense of it when the duke of Suffolk's men rode through Norwich after leaving the manor. The

both pictures: Church of St Mary, North Tuddenham, Norfolk

duke of Suffolk himself was not at Costessey, but at his estate in Claxton, several miles south-east of the city, so this was less an attempt to send a message to Norwich people (although they must have talked plenty about the three hundred armed men crossing through the city) than a practical choice of the best route there.

When the Pastons' men also left Hellesdon – barring a handful who were left to guard the manor – Daube or Sir John would have gone to Richard's house and told him the details. Richard's first concern was for Naunton. But Sir John was not like John senior, and he had little reason to worry. Indeed, not only did Sir John make efforts to get Naunton freed, and succeed – Naunton was soon back in Norwich,[4] and reported that he had been treated like a gentleman – he had behaved impressively throughout. He had not panicked, had put himself at the front of his men, and had protected the men who would have suffered if he handed them over.

This at least was promising, but nothing else was. It did not mean all the duke's men were gentlemen. They were the same kind of rabble as had attacked Gresham years earlier, and since the duke was little more in evidence than Lord Moleyns had been back then, they were no better controlled. They had not been disbanded: every day they rode from Claxton into Norwich. They made no secret what their purpose was: to grab Richard, John Daubeney and the rest.

Richard could not stay at home all day, when there was so much work to be done, but every time he left his house, to do errands in Norwich or to ride to Hellesdon or another estate, he risked running into Suffolk's men. Even a strong escort was little reassurance, when there were so many of his opponents at large.

It was inevitable they would get him before long, and it happened only a few days after Naunton was freed. He ran when he saw them, but the dozen men who had caught a glimpse chased him through the narrow streets and alleys. He knew the city well, but before long whichever way he turned he found another man in Suffolk's livery barring the way. Finally he ran out of options, backed up against a doorway, breathing hard and probably fumbling for his knife.[5] A moment's dread, then there were shouts and scuffles, and he realized help had come. Other men had seen the chase, the sheriff included. They grabbed Suffolk's men and held them back, and when they told him to run to safety, Richard did just that.[6]

The shouts followed him: we'll get you next time. We'll have you in jail. We'll see you hanged.

He can have had no doubt they meant it. And though he had friends watching out for him, he must have been conscious too that these were mostly not men with power in this situation. It was being bruited that an oyer and terminer, a commission of enquiry, was being called to look into 'all riots'. The men mentioned as its appointed leaders were the duke of Suffolk and Judge Yelverton.

The only man who could reasonably stand up to this pair, and ensure that justice was done, was the duke of Norfolk.

Although John III seems to have come and gone between Norfolk's household and the Pastons' estates, he was still the duke's man, and on good terms with him. But neither he nor his elder brother was in a position to make an offer to the duke of Norfolk that would see his lordship putting himself forward to join Yelverton and Suffolk on the panel, and firmly supporting the family and their servants when it met. Only their father could do that.

Richard probably asked both brothers to make the case to their father, and Margaret too, but he knew that this would not be enough, so he did more. He wrote himself. He must have done so knowing that John senior hated to be given advice by his estate manager, and was rarely if ever disposed to take it. But these were desperate times, and it needed a major gesture to turn things around. He spelled out to John senior what kind of gesture it needed to be. Offer Norfolk the profits of Hellesdon and Drayton, was Richard's suggestion. As he pointed out, if this was not done, both estates would almost certainly be lost to Suffolk. And if it seemed necessary, offer him more besides.

He also offered some other advice, which he surely realized would be no more welcome. Make a real attempt to bury the feud with Judge Yelverton. This too would involve negotiation. Solid offers would have to be made: Cotton, or another estate, surrendered to its claimants. Finally, the family should consider who else might be appointed to the commission, figure out which of them 'should most hurt', and make sure they were won around.

Richard did not ask this on his own account, he angled it in the way he thought would appeal most to his master. 'I beseech you to pardon of my writing', he added, 'but I have pity to see the tribulation that my mistress has here, and all your friends.'[7] This done, he waited to see if John Paston would take his advice.

He did not.

Oxnead, Norfolk

19
The rood
of the
north door

Temple Church, London

It was at about this time that John III suggested that Margery should join the duchess of Norfolk's household.[1] He had probably talked it over with Margery herself before he mentioned it to their parents, and almost certainly she welcomed the idea.

It would achieve two things, if it could be agreed. First, it would further strengthen relations with the duke and duchess and their senior servants. John III himself was needed by his family, and would be at Framlingham less in the future, so Margery could take his place as the family's liaison. The duchess was no mindless lady of fashion, she was a powerful influence on her husband. Perhaps twenty-three at this time to his twenty-one, she was the daughter of a very famous soldier of the period, John Talbot, earl of Shrewsbury. If she warmed to Margery, it could only help them all.

Second, it would get Margery away from Hellesdon, where she must have felt tense and frustrated, and was aware that she was achieving little or nothing. Unlike her brothers she could not actively defend the household, any more than she could ride round the tenants and collect the rents. The sheer intensity of the Suffolk threat had closed her life in more and more.

It was years now since the first suggestions had been made of finding her a husband, but there had been no negotiations with possible suitors over the previous few months. As she surely realized, they were unlikely to resume until things changed – which meant, until the family were confirmed in the Fastolf inheritance, and their enemies accepted that and left them in peace to enjoy it. It had been years now since Fastolf had died. It might be years more until this happened, if indeed it ever did.

Her older brothers were also making no move to marry, though the situation might well have troubled Margery more than it troubled them. Single men had a worthwhile role in life, while few single women did. She probably had more sense than to bother her mother with fretting over the problem, but perhaps she had confided in John III. Perhaps, too, she dreamed of being found a husband at Framlingham. Going to stay with an aristocratic family seemed to have worked in moving along her aunt Elizabeth's life, and there would be plenty of young men attached to the ducal household.

All these arguments clearly made sense to her mother as well. And if the Pastons pursued the scheme (which is not certain), Margery might well have visited Framlingham Castle on the great trip she made with her mother that September.

They went to London.

Though commonplace for the men of the Paston family, this was not a regular event for its women. It was probably the only time in her life that Margery visited the city, and her mother went there little if any more frequently. The idea of travelling to London must have seemed improbable when it was first mentioned, a tempting embroidered scrap which would be swept away again in the wind before she could grab hold of it. But somehow, over those weeks the threads of this little cloth wove together, and it landed in her hand. By that September, she and her mother were on the road south to the city.

To see her father was the most public of the many reasons for this visit. John senior had not come to Hellesdon or Norwich during the previous few months, and it did not look as if he would come any time soon, since he was back in prison. So – this alone must have been an extraordinary idea – they were to visit him in his cell at the famous prison of the Fleet.

The servants who did this regularly must have reassured the women that the Fleet was not like the dungeons at Norwich Castle. It was a prison well patronised by the rich and powerful, and indeed John senior was the cellmate there of Lord Henry Percy, the young son of the earl of Northumberland.[2] So Margery would meet the son of the earl of Northumberland too, except that she would meet him in jail.

She would meet her uncles William and Clement, her aunt Elizabeth and her small son. She would see the Inns of Court, and the famous Temple Church in the heart of its gardens; see St Paul's Cathedral, and perhaps go to Westminster and see the king's palace. Although there were meetings to be held, discussions to be scheduled, these were mostly for her mother. She herself might have plenty of opportunity to look around, in a city where most people did not know of the Paston family, and neither hated nor pitied them. Although everyone said you had keep your possessions close in London and watch where you put your feet, the duke of Suffolk's thugs would not follow them there. They could be free for a while of the miasma of fear.

They were escaping the pestilence too, which had come to Norwich.[3] Most likely London would be just as sweaty and stinking as Norwich in the late summer, but there would be different sights, a different smell.

Margaret and Margery would not have travelled alone. It was common for travellers to join forces for security, but if the Paston women wanted to tailor their journey to their needs – not to travel entirely by the main road and stay at the inns, but to visit one or two of their Suffolk estates, or Framlingham so that Margery could be introduced to the duchess of Norfolk – they would have taken a strong escort of their own men. The journey took two or even three days, so one or more overnight stops were unavoidable. No record survives of who travelled down to London with them, but their escort probably included one or two of their regular estate servants – perhaps Richard Calle (who certainly came back with them)[4] or John Pamping – and possibly some of the men who had been recruited to guard Hellesdon. This would have had a double benefit, since as well as keeping the women safe, it would take out of Norwich men who were facing danger there. Efforts had been continuing to counter the writs from Suffolk and their other enemies, but the situation in Norwich (and Hellesdon too) was still very uncertain.

It is quite probable that this was also the first time Margery saw Framlingham: the huge loop of the castle at the top of the hill, the smooth expanse of the mere below, and tucked into the angle made by the two, the huddled streets of the little town around its market place. She might have been admitted to the castle, curtsied to the duke and duchess, and listened as her mother discussed with the chamberlain the terms on which she might join the household. If this happened, then she and Margaret would also have gone down the hill to the grocer's shop, and paid a visit to John Calle and his family.

John Paston III had not become a friend of the Calles. As a member of the duke's household, he would not have thought it appropriate, well as he must have come to know Richard over the years. But he knew them, of course, so if he was with his mother and sister he could have made the introductions. If Richard was with them, he would naturally have done this himself.

If John senior was prone to forget that they owed much not just to Richard but to his brother as well, Margaret Paston was not. But this was not a connection that she had come to Framlingham to cultivate: it was more like her visits to the tenants in Norfolk, a necessary part of her role as John senior's wife.

The roads that linked Norwich with the towns of Suffolk, and the Suffolk towns in turn with London, were well-trodden ones across flat land. And it was late summer, a good time to travel. After a decade of unrest nothing can have been well maintained, and they would always have been wary on the way. But still, it should have been a pleasant journey.

Their first sight of London would have been of high walls, with the great spire of St Paul's and the spires and towers of the other city churches visible beyond them. Around the city to the north were market gardens, and a thin straggle of suburban houses.

They perhaps headed first for the Inns of Court. These were not within the walls, but to the west of them, between London and the king's court at Westminster: an enclave of lawyers and learning, well walled itself and guarded. To the north of the inns was the Strand, the long straight road that linked the twin cities, with its lining of big houses, and there were still larger mansions either side of the inns, on the land that led down to the Thames. The wide expanse of the river was busy with the barges and rowboats that ferried men up and downstream, and across to Southwark. The larger seagoing ships were moored at the quays farther east, but there was traffic in goods along the river well upstream of the city. The gardens of the inns stretched to the Thames, and set in them were the buildings that the lawyers of London and Westminster used as both offices and lodgings; their halls, where they ate together and discussed cases; rooms for their servants, stables, and all else that was needed in what was virtually a small city in itself.

Margery's father had treated the Inner Temple, one of several organizations that together made up the Inns, as his London base for perhaps twenty years by then, and his brothers William and Clement worked from there and probably lodged there too. The third of the Paston trio in London was Elizabeth, who was perhaps living with William at this time. Margaret and Margery's first tasks would have been the obvious ones, to meet the family and share their news.

Of all the family, Uncle William was perhaps the canniest and most successful, and Clement too seems to have established himself well as a lawyer. Even if there was a gaping hole where John senior might have sat, and a cloud of Fastolf-related worries hanging low over them, these relatives with whom Margery and her mother met up were a good way from desperation. They were family, and they honoured those ties. They all took care to keep from the sticky edges of John's quagmire, but they stayed close enough to make real efforts to pull him out of it.

That the women were in London, we know. Some other things are no more than conjecture. But we can imagine the inns in the late evening, with the scent of the last of the summer roses heavy in the air. Shuttered windows splintered with the warm gold of candlelight. Behind one of them, perhaps in a panelled parlour, a group sitting round a table, spread thick with rolls of parchment and papers, smudged, creased and torn in places, and all dense with writing. The light of the candles playing over an inkpot, quill pens, faces. A widow and a wife, both worn with care but still vigorous and lively. A girl on the cusp of womanhood, perhaps brought to London largely for this purpose. Two slick

London lawyers, and standing back in the shadows, the one servant they had been forced to trust, Richard Calle.

They had all agreed on how their family should present itself to the world: not just as gentry, but within touching distance of nobility. They had all agreed on what they had a right to possess, and taken steps to obtain the documents to prove it all. It was written up now, and needed only these last checks, to ensure the papers brought together from London, Norfolk and Suffolk told the same story, to add a last smudge and margin note, then to decide on when the papers should be presented, and how.

John III was not with them in London, but he sent down to the women with his messages and errands.[5] He had ordered a couple of pairs of hose, one black and one russet, from the hosier with the crooked back next to the Blackfriars Gate at Ludgate. He had only paid for the black hose, and had no money to spare for the other, but since he did not have a single decent pair in Norwich, he hoped the hosier would let them go on account. Perhaps Margery went with one of the servants who knew the way to Blackfriars Gate, and picked up these garments for her brother. She must have longed to buy clothes for herself too, since there was so much more choice in London than in Norwich, and if it had been agreed that she was to join the duchess of Norfolk's women she would need clothes and accessories that would fit her for this role. Money was tight – so far beyond tight it had almost loosened into irresponsibility – but if Margaret hesitated to give her some spending money, perhaps one of her uncles opened his purse. Anne would expect a gift when she got back to Hellesdon, and so would the youngest children, Walter and William, so there were trifles and probably clothes to buy for them as well.

Visiting her father was a task she might have faced more hesitantly. But if Margaret had brought her down largely so she might join the meetings over the papers, she had also brought her for this purpose: not just to cheer John senior, but to leaven the meeting between husband and wife, blunt the sharp edges of the criticisms that John was sure to make. So at least once, and probably several times, the two women and their servants made the short journey from their lodgings in or near the Inner Temple to the prison of the Fleet.

These were women used to Norwich, a big and crowded city, but London was far bigger, at least as crowded, noisier, alarming to those not familiar with its alleys and back ways. The prison was a vast block of a building, set next to the stream of the same name. This was a world from the quiet gardens and cloisters of the inns: the Fleet stream was a stinking open sewer, and the prison building seethed and swarmed with cries and outstretched hands. The prisoners were not automatically fed while in the jail, so those without resources were forced to beg at the windows for scraps of food.

John Paston was not one of these sorry souls. The wardress of the Fleet – Elizabeth Venour, a formidable woman who had become as well known as any of her charges – made her profits by selling comforts to those prisoners who could afford them, and if the Pastons could afford them only by fending off their creditors and leaving the priests at Caister to go hungry, still they made it a priority to do so. By paying, a prisoner could have a room on an upper floor, and not be confined to the stench of the dungeon. He could have his shackles removed, and even leave the jail occasionally to transact business. There was John Pamping to fetch John senior's food and bring him water to wash. And with Pamping's help he could keep in contact with the rest of his staff and his family.

The women must have discussed with William and Clement the work they were doing to get their brother freed, but there was no cause to discuss with them the business of the estate, since John senior kept all of that tight in his own hands, sending instructions out from his cell.

He was familiar with his cell by now, and must have established a routine, learned how best to handle his transactions, made friends with his noble cellmate. On this, by no means his first spell in the Fleet, he had been incarcerated for about three months when Margery and her mother visited him, and there was no immediate prospect of his being freed. The Fleet was primarily a prison for debtors and those who had defaulted in court cases, and although it is not clear exactly what the case was against John Paston at this point, it probably involved both debt and defaults.

Margaret had had enough of his letters – and Margery would have heard enough from her mother – that both of them were probably braced for a torrent of grumbles and grouches. John Paston had always seen his problems as someone else's fault. If Margery bought so much as a petticoat, she would have avoided showing it off to her father, for fear of being scolded for extravagance. But although there were old arguments, old problems that had to be raked over, the women must have been anxious to show a cheerful face, and perhaps John was as well.

As well as the crises, there were positive things they could bring up. The evidences were one of them: they would be public knowledge soon, so their existence could be discussed, though the Pastons would have alluded only very obliquely to exactly how they had been assembled. There were useful steps that had been taken in Norfolk, too. Richard Calle had spoken to the high sheriff, and Margaret had been round the Pastons' old friends and relatives, sounding them out and trying to put together a list of people she and her family could rely on.[6] It was a list of modest gentry, rather than of the rich and powerful, and the duke of Norfolk did not figure on it.

John's appearance might have shocked them both. He was not an old man: he was only forty-four. But he was a man who had never found it easy to rise above the stresses of his life, and by this time he was probably in fragile health. If Margaret longed for help in facing the problems

London

All Saints Church, Welbourne, Norfolk

at Hellesdon, at Cotton, at Caister, she must have realized it was not going to come from her husband.

The legal enquiries were still going on into Fastolf's will, and several times John had been taken to Mistress Venour's house, and given evidence there to the investigators. He probably claimed to be confident that in time the case would be proved in his favour; and the women probably reassured him that they were confident of this too. Once they were let out the door the smiles and false assurances would have been left behind, as they travelled back wreathed in worry to their lodgings.

John III had sent one other message to his sister. She would see the sights on this trip, as well as she could between the working sessions and visits to her father, and one he advised her not to miss was the abbey church of St Saviour in Bermondsey.[7] The famous Rood of Grace, the Saxon cross set in the north door, was where women traditionally prayed that the Lord might send them a good husband. Go there, he wrote to Margery, and pray that one will be found for you.

It was a suggestion that was most likely given to every young girl of marriageable age who came to London, but perhaps John knew it would resonate particularly with Margery. There was little practical he could do to help her, but he could offer her his sympathy along with his little demands for errands. Nor was this advice only sympathy: they must both have at least half-believed in the powers such prayers had to make things happen, though not always quite in the way the person praying had envisaged.

This was one suggestion Margaret could readily agree to, so most likely the two women made the trip together. Perhaps Elizabeth came with them too. It was a good walk to the abbey, so they would have picked a fine day to head down to the ferry pier and take a boat across to Southwark. This area to the south of the Thames, well known for its stews (its brothels), inns and bear gardens, was where Fastolf had had his London mansion. The Pastons had probably lost it to a rival claimant several years earlier.

A long gravel road led the half-mile or so south from the Southwark moorings, down the bustle of Borough High Street, past the great church of St Olave's, and over the fields to the abbey. In those days it was an isolated place, but the abbey church was one of the largest and most famous in London, so there was a steady flow of worshippers taking the path. Catherine of Valois, Henry V's widow, had lived out her last days in the monastery, twenty years earlier. Like the Temple Church with its ancient effigies at the heart of the Inns of Court, this had been a haunt of the Knights Templar, the great order of martial knights that had been disbanded long before.

Beggars at the door; nuns inside who looked for alms (and were given them). A blackened-oak door, with the cross centuries old set high above it. The aged, the lame, young girls like Margery, and widows like Elizabeth too, coming to worship the relics, to think over their own lives, their hopes, their fears, and to pray that good fortune might turn their way.

Elizabeth might also have given her niece some bracing advice. Don't stay at home with your mother too long; don't let your hopes curdle. Don't wait for a good time for your marriage to be planned, as the family sees it: if you do, that time might never come. The prayers that come true are the ones that people seize and run with. Chances are, Margery, that is what you will need to do.

Church of St Lawrence, Little Waldingfield, Suffolk,

20
Nail his
ear

Castle Acre Priory, Norfolk

Richard was with the women for some of their time in London – they were there for a week or two at most – and for the first part of their journey north again.[1] It was probably as long as he and Margery had ever spent in each other's company.

Her mother was with them, of course. Margaret was firmly in charge of the agenda, but Richard probably made the arrangements. And as Margery could see, her mother relied on him not just for this, but to accompany her on her visit to the sheriff of Sudbury – where they stopped to deliver writs drawn up by the London Pastons – and to introduce her to some of the family's Suffolk tenants and estate workers.

They went from Sudbury to Cotton. By now the days were drawing in and the leaves drifting down to the ditches. The estate was still under dispute. The hall seems to have been empty. It must have been desolate, with the broken-down bridge, the lead missing from the roof, probably no more done to repair the place than was needed to keep out the worst of the rain. Perhaps they did not stay in this miserable wreck, because John III (who joined them after they arrived at Cotton) wrote later from Hempnall Hall, another of the moated manors on the estate.[2]

The purpose of their brief stay at Cotton was to get an update on the situation on this and other nearby estates, contact the tenants and reinforce the message that whatever others might tell them these were Paston lands, make arrangements to collect the rent as soon as the Michaelmas due date was past, and hold a court. Margery and her mother stayed at their base while Richard rode off to see Edward Dale. He came back with the news that Jenney and his men were planning to hold their own court on the nearby (and also disputed) estate of Calcott.

So the peace of London was firmly behind them, and they were back facing the need to fight if they were to hold on to their lands. They would need men not just to secure their own court, but to disrupt their rivals' one, and they would have to stay longer at Cotton than they had first planned.

When John III arrived, with a group of men from Hellesdon, he sat down with Richard and Margaret – perhaps Margery listened in too – to consider what resources they needed (and what they could afford), and how best to use them. Richard reckoned Jenny might muster as many as 300 men, so they needed to find something approaching this number.

The plans made, John III and Richard put them into practice. A messenger was sent to Norwich, to tell John Daubeney to bring all the men who could be spared from Hellesdon and Drayton. John III rode off to Framlingham, and asked to borrow some of the duke's household men. He enlisted a colleague called John Wickes, apparently a gentleman of some resource and standing, who helped to gather together more men when they stopped at Caister en route. Richard meanwhile talked to his old friends on the farms, persuading the tenants to add to the numbers. Within days they had put together around 300 men.

Once all these were assembled, a group under Daubeney and Wickes rode off to wait as secretly as they could at Calcott, planning to show themselves just in time to disrupt Jenney's plans and scare off his supporters. Margery and her mother must have had a frustrating time waiting at Cotton till someone returned to tell them what happened, but when they got back Daubeney and his colleagues gave them a hilarious account of the chases through the Suffolk lanes that followed the meeting of the two rival groups, and the actions they took afterwards, moving all the tenants' animals off the estate so there would be nothing for Jenney's men to distrain. The Paston men had held off holding their own court in the wake of their opponents' threats, but they had succeeded in driving away Yelverton and Jenney's men.

By this time, though, their opponents had sent to the duke of Norfolk with protests. John III might be one of the duke's liveried retainers, but so were some of his opponents. The duke must have realized he had made a mistake in letting John III borrow men for such a purpose, and he demanded that both sides disband their men and let a neutral person supervise the estates until the issues were resolved.

The Pastons had to disband the men anyway, because they could not afford to pay so many for long, or to leave Hellesdon and Drayton stripped bare, but as Richard probably pointed out, they might as well gather in some rent before they did so. So John III stalled before responding to the duke's messenger for as long as he felt he could without infuriating the duke (who was heading off to London anyway), claiming he could agree nothing without consulting his mother, and meanwhile Richard handed out rent books, and the men went around the farms and cottages collecting rent and distraining goods from those who would not pay.

Margery must have watched all this activity, and she probably found it entertaining: the Paston women were never under threat, and Daube and Richard made a joke of all the hiding under hedges and the frantic rush to haul in the silver before John III promised the duke they would stop their activity. But underneath the laughter and the bustle, she must have known that none of this was bringing this the family any closer to safety and security.

The high jinks in Suffolk had delayed them long enough that when Margery and her mother got back to Norwich, a letter from John senior, written after they had left London, was already waiting for them.[3] There was page after page of it, close written. The advice John Paston gave was most of it useless or worse. He had barely been in East Anglia for months, and had no real idea what the men were doing. There was a jarring contrast between the camaraderie of Cotton, and John senior's demands that his wife double-check on Richard Calle and the rest, for fear they were cheating or slacking.

He wanted some winter woollens. Could Margaret please find out where his brother William had got his tippet from, he wrote, since the fine worsted in that would do well, if the price was right. And it would be good to have worsted, the local cloth, 'for worship of Norfolk'. Perhaps he meant to be funny. Perhaps he knew what a forlorn figure he had cut in his cell, and was trying to cheer up his wife and daughter.

At the end of the letter he broke into rhyme:

Item, I shall tell you a tale
Pamping and I have picked your mail
and taken out pieces five
for upon trust of Calle's promise we may soon thrive.
And if Calle bring us hither twenty pound
you shall have your pieces again good and round
or else if he will not pay you the value of the pieces there
to the post do nail his ear,
or else do him some other sorrow,
for I will no more in his default borrow;
and if but the receiving of my livelihood be better plied,
he shall Christ's curse and mine clean tried.
And look you be merry and take no thought,
for this rhyme is cunningly wrought.
My Lord Percy and all this house
recommend them to you, dog, cat and mouse,
and wish that you had been here still,
for they say you are [a] good girl.
No more to you at this time.
But God him save that made this rhyme.

This might have gone down better with Margery if it had not been so mean about Richard Calle.

Church of St Mary, North Tuddenham, Norfolk

21
Your
featherbeds

Norwich
Cathedral

The news that greeted Richard when he got back to Norwich was that the duke of Suffolk's agent had ordered searches of the court registries, going back a hundred years or more, to try to prove who had bought Hellesdon and Drayton manors, and when.[1] It was said he had turned up evidence to strengthen the duke of Suffolk's claims. No surprise there, then. The previous agent, Master Philip, had moved on, and the bailiff of Eye (a small town in Suffolk), a man called Bottesford, was taking charge of the heavy end of the duke's activities. There were even more men than before assembled at Claxton and Costessey, and it was evident that next time they came to Hellesdon, they would not turn around at the gate and ride back again empty handed.

Richard probably moved into the chantry at Hellesdon Hall, and certainly made plans, with Sir John, Daubeney and the rest, to shift the Pastons' main defences back to the Wensum valley. John Wickes, the man who had played a hand with Daubeney at Calcott, came up to Hellesdon with some of his men. Sir John Paston was in charge, and the others were maybe glad to let him take the lead.

The men might have moved many of the cattle and the plough horses to the family's other estates, though they chose to leave the sheep in the meadows: there must have been little grazing left for them on the other lands, or perhaps Sir John was reluctant to spare the men to drive them off. They rode round the villagers and the tenant farmers. They persuaded the parson to store some of the furnishings from the hall – they would be safer in the parsonage – and another tenant farmer to do the same. Meanwhile Margaret went to men in Norwich and beyond, asking what the duke of Suffolk and his men were doing, and what was happening with the writs. Sir John Heveningham had had a hand in the lawsuits, and she spoke to him. Richard must have hoped she would take the advice that her husband had ignored, and offer the man a decent bribe. But it seemed the duke's men had already got to him, and he was now nothing but a 'dogbolt'.[2]

Spider season, a damp autumn. And the duke of Suffolk, furred with enmity, was weaving his sticky web to snare them.

It must have seemed unwise for the women to stay at Hellesdon, but almost equally unwise for them to leave. The place had become their home, anyway. Margery was there in mid-October 1465 when a group of the duke of Suffolk's men rode over the water meadows and up to the house. The message they brought was simple: this land is not yours. It's proven now that it belongs to the duke. You should leave it right away.

That was not how Sir John saw it, or any of them. There was an altercation of sorts: Richard and Wickes put a note together about it afterwards, and other people added to it too, less good scribes. One of them might have been Margery herself. When they had finished it was still none too clear exactly what happened, but clear that they all saw it as an assault on Margery and her brother. It had terrified them both.[3]

And that was only the warning. If they ignored it more men would come, and force the Pastons out.

So they perhaps half-ignored it. The grooms kept the horses ready, and the family moved a few of their possessions to Norwich, but kept their personal things at the hall, and continued to live there. When the word came that the duke's men were on their way in force, and they rode off in a hurry, Margery had to leave behind her sewing things – gold trim, silk, thread – and her ivory looking glass and comb. Richard left his books and some of his papers. Sir John stayed behind with a small group to confront the attackers, but there was nothing to be said for the rest of them being arrested by the duke's men, or standing in the yard as Margaret had done at Gresham while the house was torn apart around them. They would have reached the shelter of the woods, or one of the side tracks to Norwich – not the road on which Suffolk's men came – before the troops got to the manor.

Church of St Catherine, Ludham, Norfolk

What had happened after they left Hellesdon? Both Margery and her family, and Richard and his colleagues, would have been impatient for news. It was days before they heard from Sir John, or gained any idea where he had gone (or been taken). However some of the other men who had stayed with him got to Norwich after Suffolk's men had gone. They could not have stayed at Hellesdon Hall any longer, because nothing was left of it but a heap of rubble.[4]

Margery and her family had expected it to be bad, but it was worse than that, worse than anything they had envisaged. Five hundred men had come, armed and ready for trouble, scattering the sheep and rabbits, churning up the mud in the water meadows. They had begun by demolishing the main house, the buttery, the brewhouse, the kitchens. A group of them had made for the warreners' lodge, and wrecked that as well. By the time they were done at the lode they had learned there was an armoury in the church, the handguns and bows that Sir John had assembled back in the summer, so they ran to the church, and set about vandalizing that. (They threw out the old parson, ignoring his pleas, though they did not hurt him.) They found goods that Richard, Wickes and the rest had put there for safekeeping – Wickes had had a silver collar, livery he had been given by the king, but he never saw that again – and stole the lot. They were wild enough by this time, high on the drug of violence, perhaps drunken too, that men climbed on the high altar, waving their swords and shouting out their triumph. They smashed the images, kicked over the cross, turned the steeple to firewood.[3] Men rampaged through every house in the village, not once but five or six times each, till they had found every last hiding place, nicked every last farthing.

It was worse than an invasion by the French.

The first rampage done, the bulk of the men rode off, but a gang led by Bottesford returned at midnight, and raided the parsonage by torchlight. They demanded to know whether any of the furnishings belonged to the Pastons. A terrified parson, or his cook, must have told them. They loaded up a cart with feather beds and kitchen vessels, then went to the other house outside the village where things had been left, and did the same. Then come dawn, the troops rode back through Hellesdon and Drayton, on their way to the duke of Suffolk's estate at Costessey, and contingents of them were dispatched to the tenants, to demand that they send their men to help. Grumbling perhaps, but too scared to resist, the farm labourers of Hellesdon and Drayton had to help load up the carts, as the duke's men proceeded to carry off everything they could from the Pastons' houses: the lead from the roofs, the iron pipes, the door, the gates. Wooden beams and anything else that was too large to move they hacked to pieces.

The next day Suffolk's men were back, and the next, scouring the fields for men they could accuse of having helped the Pastons. Bottesford and the bailiff of Costessey organized gangs of men who drove off all the livestock that had remained at Hellesdon, and Drayton too: six hundred hogs, eight hundred ewes, four hundred lambs. They would probably have take the rabbits if they could only have rounded them up, and the fish out of the stewponds. They found the Pastons' cook, Davy Arnold, and a couple of other men, and dragged them off to jail: not in Norwich, where appalled rumours were whipping round the streets, and even Sir John Heveningham might have protested, but in the Suffolk town of Eye, territory the duke had under firm control.

Once Suffolk's troops were also back under firm control, their master led them through the city gates and along the streets of Norwich. He had not been present for the raid, but he meant to enforce his will in its aftermath, perhaps even more so because he knew that what had happened had turned many men and women against him. There were plenty of people in the city who would have kept silent while the Pastons were dispossessed of the old Fastolf lands, and not asked too carefully how the duke of Suffolk had managed to prove title to them, but they could not ignore the desecration of the church. Probably the duke was appalled at that himself, but now it was done, he chose to use his power in the region to support those who had done it. He was not the man his father had been, a valued counsellor of the king; his character was smaller and meaner, his actions cold and selfish.

The duke's men settled in a strong guard round Suffolk Inn – his palace in the city – and messengers rode to order the mayor, aldermen and sheriffs to attend on his grace. In the hours and days that followed the troops made arrests on the streets, 'in the king's name', as they announced to those with nerve enough to witness it.

Richard was not arrested, as far as we know, or any of the Pastons' chief servants, so they must have fled from the city, or found friends to hide them during this period of terror.

Over the chill days that followed, a stream of men and women rode down the valley road and past the Hellesdon mills. They went to the site of the hall, and looked for themselves at the chaos that was all that remained of the strong stone house. They went up the hill to the church, and stared at the ruin it had become.[5] The Paston family made the journey too.

The parson had friends; the warreners, the shepherds, the brewer had friends. The men who had laboured under the soldiers' whips to shift the stone and brick onto the carts had friends. A ripple of outrage spread out from Hellesdon across the county. Even William Jenney, it was rumoured, reckoned the people of Hellesdon had been hard done by.

Many women would have been driven to despair by this, huddled by their autumn fire and wept at the unkindness of fate. Not Margaret Paston. She had faced down adversity before, and she did it now. With her to push them, her children and her servants followed suit.

As far as is known, Margery did not leave her mother and join the duchess of Norfolk's household. Bravely as she might be taking it, her mother had been shaken to the core, and so surely had she. They needed each other, and the faces of their long-established friends and servants around them. They needed, too, the sympathy of those who had gawked at the ruins and the splintered church steeple. Perhaps this could be used; perhaps the sheer horror of it would cauterize the old wounds that had festered for so long.

There was work to be done as well. They could not expect ever to gain compensation for all the damage, but they could and must file claims in the courts. Richard and John

Wickes were ordered to draw up an inventory of everything that was gone. They went round the men and women who had been at Hellesdon, asking them what of theirs was lost. Margery's mirror, her comb, her sewing thread; John Wickes' black fustian doublet, his grey horse and its harness; Sir John's side morrey gown, his black satin doublet, his staff and his book in French. Richard must have minded his own losses almost as bitterly as Margery resented hers. His possessions were so similar to Sir John's as to make them sound like twins: a side morrey gown, a black satin doublet, a staff, a book in French.[5]

It must have been a cold winter for all of them.

Margery never saw her father alive again.

Nor did her mother, most likely, though word of how he was faring would have come regularly from London, as the horses bearing the Paston's servants and agents ploughed through the mud of the roads that winter. The answer was, not well. Up in Norfolk they had all survived the onslaught, and kept standing. But in his prison cell, the news must have destroyed John senior.

It was he who had brought all this down on his family. And perhaps that winter, it occurred to him more than once that he should never have done so.

Too late now. Too late to renounce the Fastolf estates; too late to regain his own health, his vigour, his optimism. All that was now gone to rubble as frost-rimed as the stones of Hellesdon Hall. At some point, it seems, his brothers managed to get him out of the Fleet. All it meant was that he died a free man.

May 1466: the cold winter over, the nightmare of the attacks on Hellesdon over. A spring, if not a very optimistic one. King Edward IV still shakily holding his throne, and the Paston family still shakily holding on to some, at least, of the Fastolf inheritance. Sir John and his brother John III, young men with energy and determination, leading the battle; and the Paston servants, most of them, still loyal. Although Margaret Paston was still struggling on, her husband's death must have killed something in the core of her. But there was a new great task to be tackled now. Her husband had to be buried.

And Margaret was determined that he should be buried splendidly. Her elder sons probably agreed. They were both of them sick of darned hose and frustrated creditors and account books and the petty economies their father had insisted on. It was Sir John's task now to establish the great place in East Anglian society that his father had never quite managed to fill. So this could be the beginning: the men of Norfolk and Suffolk, gathering

Church of St Mary Magdalene, Debenham, Suffolk

together not just to mourn John senior, but to bury a mound of enmity with him, and if all went well, to continue the process that had begun with the Hellesdon attack, and look a little more kindly on his sons.

He had died in London, but they must all have agreed that he had to be buried in Norfolk.[1] However fine a job the Pastons had done in compiling their genealogy, they could not point to a church under whose flagstones lay the bones of generations of wealthy and respected ancestors. In Mautby Margaret's family had that, but John Paston was not a Mautby. The judge, John senior's father, had been buried in the Lady Chapel of Norwich Cathedral. Perhaps the family considered burying John there; perhaps they considered the church at Paston, or – though it was smallish, as Norwich churches went – St Peter Hungate in the city. They could have considered the chapel at Caister, where seven priests and seven poor men were still diligently singing for the soul of Sir John Fastolf, but Fastolf himself had not been buried there, and it was not the right size for the great funeral the family was determined on.

Their choice fell on Bromholm Priory, the religious foundation a short walk from Paston village. The papers the Pastons had submitted to the king had shown a descent from William de Glanville, who was reliably believed to have founded Bromholm three and a half centuries earlier. It was near to Paston, Gresham and Oxnead; they had a solid connection with it, no contemporary great family claimed it as theirs, and if they wanted to establish a burial place for future generations, there were worse options than to begin now at Bromholm.

We must hope the undertakers did a good job of the embalming, because it was a week after John Paston's death before all of this was agreed, and a funeral procession set out from London to Bromholm. Twelve poor men, bearing torches, walked in front of the coffin. The London-based family, priests who had a connection with the Pastons, servants and others (including paid mourners) would have followed on behind. Funeral processions move slowly: it took them six days to get there.

Just as she could not reasonably have left for Framlingham after the Hellesdon attack, Margery could not have joined the duchess of Norfolk's household before her father's funeral, or during the months of mourning that followed. Any finery she had bought in London must have been packed away, if it had not been stolen, and she had to resign herself to staying by her mother's side.

Neither she nor the children of the family would have gone to London and joined the mourning procession, and probably their mother did not go either. They more likely stayed in Norwich until John's corpse was brought to the city en route to Bromholm. It was set in state, probably in St Peter Hungate, and the family paid for thirty-eight priests to sing dirges over the coffin while the men and women of Norwich filed past to pay their respects. Thirty-nine children, dressed in surplices made for the occasion, stood in rows and sang alongside the priests inside and outside the church. The glaziers were called in: a couple of the church windows were taken out so that the smoke from the torches could escape during the service, and afterwards were reinstalled.

Thirty-eight priests. Some of the Pastons' creditors – Richard Calle was one, they were way behind with his wages, and it looked unlikely that the balance would be made up any time soon – might have widened their eyes at that. Those who remembered Margaret

Paston asking Lady Morley how she ought to behave might have whispered behind their hands that she had not gained a sense of proportion since. This was the kind of grandiose send-off that would have suited a great captain of war, or a duke, or at a pinch an esteemed judge. Everyone knew that John Paston senior had been none of those things. But for all he might have thought it unwise, Richard would probably not have scoffed. He maybe reckoned that Margaret needed this, that in a sense all of the family needed it. Harsh reality would set back in soon enough. They could first have their June of drama and pomp.

And they did. The procession from Norwich to Paston was even larger than the procession to Norwich. The family probably went with it, although Richard and the other senior servants would have been too busy making the arrangements to walk alongside them. There were representatives from the family estates, members of all the four orders of friars who had establishments in Norwich, bell ringers, the poor men with their torches, a woman to tend the corpse and stop it from stinking, four more 'keepers of the corpse' and thirty-six clerks. Plus more distant relations, business connections, friends, patrons: a huge cross-section of people from Norwich, from places across Suffolk and Norfolk, and some from well beyond.

There was nowhere for all the mourners to lodge at Bromholm, an isolated place, and it was too far from Norwich for them to get back to the city that night, so tents were hired for them to sleep in.

Bromholm is within brine and seagull distance of the North Sea. It sits in flat fields that stretch to a wide horizon. Its fame lay in its cross, made out of fragments of the True Cross of Christ, that had been brought to England in 1223 by an English priest who had been at Constantinople. It had had a mention in *Piers Plowman*, and another in Chaucer's Reeve's tale: it had been a magnet for generations of pilgrims, kings and queens among them.[3]

Even in June the north Norfolk coast can be chilly, and a funeral sets a cool edge on the brightest day. But the flowers would have been out in the hedgerows, the rooks cawing in the trees as the long, long procession wound its way down the lanes from Paston village and out to the monastery. Through the great gateway, into the monastery close, then through the huge door and into the church, where the coffin, covered in cloth of gold, was set in state for the funeral service. It was held on 3 or 4 June 1466.

Cold knees on the stone floor, and a long solemn service. And after, the feast, for which the victuals ordered included geese, capons, chickens, pigs, calves and lambs. There was fish too; there were eggs, gallons of milk and cream, four pints of butter, and huge quantities of ale to wash it all down. The women of the family would have had little part in the service, but they would have been at the feast, receiving the condolences of their relatives, friends, and enemies too, and the sanctimonious advice of the priors and parsons.

Some things would change now, and any change could hardly be for the worse. If Margery sincerely mourned her father, perhaps most of all at this time she felt hope.

A light was left on the grave, and continued to burn thereafter. The monks of Bromholm were paid for this, of course, and the Pastons also paid the vicar of Dalling to set out for Rome, and bring back a pardon 'to pray for all our friends' souls'.[2] It cost them eight shillings and fourpence – not much for such a long journey, so perhaps the vicar had other commissions too – and they bought him a black gown to wear, which cost them another eight shillings.

At the time, Margaret meant a great tomb to be built to house her husband's bones. The same had been intended for his father the judge, but it had never been built. It had been Fastolf's intention, and mostly likely was never achieved for him either. It was perhaps to no one's surprise that stonemasons did not turn up at Bromholm Priory, and the cloth of gold sat on top of the coffin till it began to fray and then disintegrate.[3]

Bromholm Priory, Norfolk

23
Sufficiently
declared

A new master: and considering how the old master had behaved in the last years of his life, Richard Calle was probably not unhappy about that. It meant a period of uncertainty and adjustment, nevertheless. He had to answer now to a man several years younger than him, and much less experienced in managing the family estates than either Richard or John senior. He had to pass on his knowledge, without ever making the mistake of telling Sir John what to do. And he had to cope too with the fact that where John senior had managed his affairs in microscopic detail, his son took a much more general view of them. He was no more inclined to travel round and meet the tenants now than he had been a few years earlier. He spent most of his time down south: not at the Inns of Court, but at the king's court at Westminster. Richard probably found himself travelling down the road to London more frequently in these months than he had ever done before.

Back in Norwich, it was not only Richard who had to contend with changes in the household. It must have been hard most of all for Margaret. For years she had worked as intensely, and at times almost as obsessively, as her husband. Now she had only Gresham and Mautby as her own, and her son could – and did – sideline her when he chose over the administration of the rest. Her son could also sideline the servants she and his father had chosen, and show his favour to the men he preferred. It was tough for Father Gloys: at one point Sir John called him a 'proud, peevish and evil-disposed priest',[1] which speaks plenty about pleas made and pleas ignored.

Above, Church of St Andrew, Bacton, Norfolk
Right, Elm Hill, Norwich

Richard was damned if he too would be sidelined, though he probably had to worry less than most. He was not in the same position as Daube; not a carousing companion of Sir John. But in running the estates he was all but indispensable, and he knew it. He watched his back, even so, and took care to build up his support in other quarters. Indeed, he put so much effort into courting William Paston that it backfired and angered Margaret. He was not helped by the fact that someone – Gloys perhaps, or another nervous man looking to profit from the change in control, and to push Richard down the ladder in the process – told on him to Margaret. She wrote to Sir John to warn him about Richard and 'his fellow' (that is, one of the men working for him) – and by implication, his uncle too. Richard had 'nigh conquered' William, as she put it, 'with fair promises touching his livelihood and other things'.[2] Even if Richard did not see the letter – perhaps he did, Sir John was perfectly capable of playing people off against each other – he will have sensed what was going on, and he did not like it.

It was clear why things were so tight and tense. Everyone, from the most open-handed to the meanest of the family and their servants, was necessarily focused on the tricky issue of money. However Richard looked at the situation, it must have been apparent to him that although the Pastons might appear rich to more humble folks, they simply did not have enough of it.

The duke of Suffolk had slunk away after his display of bravado in Norwich: he had realized, if slowly, how badly the Hellesdon attack had gone down, not just in the city but in Westminster too, and it seems he made no attempt to consolidate his hold on the land. But that did not alter the fact that even if they were firmly regained the Hellesdon and

Drayton estates would take years to recover, and that there was no prospect of rebuilding their manor houses. So much of the Fastolf inheritance had leached away, and so much of what the family still held precariously on to was ravaged by attacks from their enemies.

Sir John was not making money from legal clients, as his father had done (albeit less successfully than his own father). He was spending it instead on making a fine display at court. He had to pay the funeral expenses, the bills for the men who had been hired to guard Hellesdon and Cotton; at some point he would have to make up the backlog of wages and deal with his (and his brother John III's) long-standing creditors in London. It was not apparent where he would find the money to do these things.

Nor could he lay claim himself to everything his father had (more or less) owned. Margaret had her chunk, and was showing every sign of keeping it just as close as Agnes Paston still kept hers. And as had happened after the judge's death, a new generation of heirs were grappling to obtain their share (and more) of a fractured and complex estate. John III, Margery, the younger children: none of them were as sly and cunning as their father had been, but all of them needed to be reassured that they would not be left beached and breathless in the wake of their big brother's careless extravagance. The older generation of William, Clement and Elizabeth had not forgotten the wrangles over the judge's will, or the promises that had been made by John senior when he moved on the Fastolf lands, and not yet fulfilled. Just as John senior had found himself pressed at times to maintain the lifestyle of his father while sharing his father's estate with all the other claimants to it, so his eldest son would have to find a way of fulfilling his own expensive ambitions with a fraction of what his father had left – or going broke, and learning the hard way to trim his ambitions back down.

But if money was the biggest problem, in other ways the situation over the next few months must have seemed more hopeful than it had been for years. A death such as John Paston's signals the end of more than a body; it also provided an opportunity for old quarrels to be buried. It became apparent that Sir John was motivated to put them behind him, and had a better sense than his father had ever had of what he must do to achieve this. Part of what he had to do was surely financial, and added still further to his money worries, but part was not. Courtesy and charm could unravel many tight knots.

Whatever gestures Sir John needed to make, he must have made them, because in the months after his father's death the snarled string of the court cases slowly unravelled. By August of the following year,[3] probate was at last granted in Fastolf's will. The executors were Sir John himself and Thomas Howes, so he probably made efforts both with Howes, and with other men Fastolf had named, who agreed to withdraw their claim to participate. Caister, and many of the other estates that had been Fastolf's, fell securely into his hands – and the investment he had made must have been repaid almost immediately.

No more was heard of Fastolf's nephews, so perhaps they were dead, and if not, they were paid off.

Church of St Catherine, Ludham, Norfolk

Sir John even managed to sidestep the obligation to continue to leave a chunk of the castle to the priests and the poor men, and to put up with the dirges echoing from the castle chapel. One of the powerful men who facilitated this was William Waynflete, bishop of Winchester, who had been involved from the outset in the negotiations over the estate. He came to a deal with Sir John whereby the money for the college at Caister, which had never got its licence, albeit it had been operating after a fashion for years, would be diverted instead to Waynflete's new college at Oxford. Fastolf might have a memorial there, masses could be said at the college chapel: it would benefit Waynflete, benefit the Pastons, and since Fastolf was long dead, it was immaterial whether it benefited him.[4]

He did less well with Judge Yelverton. That must have become a bitter and personal quarrel, and it was not only with John senior: the tussles at Cotton were not forgotten. Yelverton did not reconcile himself to the Pastons winning the war he had fought against them for so long. He kept some men on his side, not surprisingly – he was a powerful man, and he had a fair point. So there were battles still to be fought over several of the Suffolk estates, but even so, things were far sunnier than they had been a year before.

In this, and much else, John Paston senior had laid the foundations of a mansion he never dwelled in. The papers and rolls of parchment that the Pastons had worked so hard to assemble were probably delivered to the court before his death, but it was after it – only weeks after it – that King Edward pronounced on the content of the documents. He took them to be what the Pastons intended them to be seen as, 'writing of old hand and ... old testaments and evidences'. The king's 'trusty and wellbeloved knight Sir John Paston', his uncle William and his uncle Clement (no mention was made of the women of the family) were found to be 'gentlemen descended lineally of worshipful blood since the Conquest'. No man could now claim that the Pastons were bondmen whose estates could be disputed; and since Sir John intended to make his home at Caister, the king pronounced, his neighbours were to be friendly and supportive to him.[5]

Was the long nightmare finally ended? Could the Pastons and their servants hope to live now in a country that was at peace, at peace with their neighbours and with each other? For a while, at least, they must have believed it would happen.

More might happen; lives that had been held suspended might now move forwards. None of the new generation of Pastons had married, but Sir John and John III were now well into their twenties; it was time they were settled, and by 1467, the year after John senior's death, they were writing to each other about the possibilities. William set about getting himself a wife too, and at around this time he made a splendid match, with Lady Anne Beaufort, a daughter of the duke of Somerset, a woman with royal blood in her veins. Those of their friends and neighbours (and old enemies too) who took in how thoroughly the family's position had changed were soon writing to Margery's brothers with suggestions of the marriage she too might make.[6]

But by this time she had perhaps already chosen a different path for herself.

24
Pleasure and profit

Church of All Saints, Edingthorpe, Norfolk

Richard Calle was probably in his early thirties in 1467. He had been working for the Paston family for at least fifteen years, growing from a young lad who watched at the shoulders of older men to the family's leading man of business. He had left the servants' hall long before, and had a house of his own. He almost certainly carried out some business transactions on his own account, as well as those he did for his employers. Even if his wages were being paid well in arrears, he must have had money in his coffers. He had not married young, but it was high time now that he found himself a wife. Likeable, intelligent, successful in his career, solvent: he was in a good position to win a fine woman, and he knew it.

Margery Paston was perhaps seventeen. Many girls of her class and era were betrothed, and often married too, far younger than this. Her family had been talking, if desultorily, of finding her a husband for several years. She was more than ready to step out of her mother's shadow and run a household herself.

It is unlikely that anyone suggested to Richard that he might look at Margery as a potential wife, though, and equally unlikely that anyone suggested to Margery that she might look at Richard. The gap in their ages was no more than a small part of this; the rest of it lay in the complex mesh of status signals that told men and women of this time what kind of match they might look to make.

Her uncle married a duke's daughter. Her eldest brother too was talking of finding a wife with connections to the royal court. Even those who had chosen to forget John senior's questionable dealings might have murmured that this was somewhat over-optimistic. Whatever front the Pastons displayed, they did not really have deep-rooted connections with the aristocracy. They had been, and in some ways they still were, the kind of provincial gentry family whose members (or at least, some of them) were not entirely comfortable with the manners of the court; and a man who knew about their financial affairs would have been well aware that the income from their estates did not yet, and perhaps never would, stretch to cover a lifestyle on this grand scale.

But it was what Sir John Paston wanted, that was clear. And he not only wanted it, he had persuaded other men (at court, though perhaps not so many in Norfolk) that it was what he deserved.

What he and his family wanted for Margery was not the same. Nor was this a question of selling her off cheap, as her grandmother had airily suggested a few years earlier: it reflected the pragmatic fact that Margery was not in the same bargaining position as her eldest brother, the family's main heir. All families with land and money encompass a range of individuals with a range of affluence, and in the nature of these things Sir John was at the top of the Paston scale and Margery somewhere towards the bottom.

There was no prospect of her inheriting a fortune, so she could not realistically expect the kind of husband that an heiress might attract. The same was true of her sister Anne, and of all her other brothers. Unless a person in their kind of situation was exceptionally successful (as Uncle William undoubtedly was), the aristocracy was not where they needed to aim. The money that a woman in Margery's position could expect to have settled on her by her family on her marriage would get her a husband of the middling sort: a man with a house and some land, a decent but not vast income, the ability to keep a wife in comfort and retain a few servants; a man with the respect of other men of standing in the county, but not a man who looked to chat with kings.

Three hundred marks a year: that was the figure that had attracted Agnes Paston's interest. In 1467 or thereabouts, John Strange wrote to Margery's brother suggesting his nephew as a suitable husband.[1] The boy would have a small jointure and an inherited income of 200 marks a year. The difference between 200 and 300 marks probably does not reflect any diminution in Margery's bargaining position, it simply gives a rough indication of the range of wealth that her family expected of her future husband.

Money was much talked about – and figured even more in what was written about – but it was not, of course, the only consideration. The intangibles of society weighed heavily too. Her husband was expected to come from a family not dissimilar to her own, and probably to be in a position within it not dissimilar to her own: a younger son, most likely, whose older brother had aspirations not unlike her brother's. This would settle her in a social position with which she would be familiar and in which she would be comfortable; it was how the country's gentry knitted their fabric.

What she could expect; or rather, what a woman in a similar position in a family superficially similar to her own could expect. Because Margery had not been found a husband. It was by no means too late for her to do so, but she must have had a sense of what her family was doing for her, and what its outcome might prove to be. She must have been conscious of that as her grandmother bantered with Master Wrothe, as her big brother John III suggested she should pray to the Rood of Grace, as Sir John Strange wrote his letter, and her brother Sir John quite likely mentioned to her that he had received this approach. She was probably painfully aware that properly planned negotiations did not begin in a cack-handed way, or fizzle out like a pissed-on log.

She was conscious of what had happened to Elizabeth too. The years of battling with her mother, the stream of unsuitable suggestions that were never really taken up, the time passing and prospects fading. Was there a danger that the same might happen to her?

She quite likely believed there was.

It was by no means certain that the size of jointure that Master Wrothe and Master Strange expected her to receive would actually be committed to by her brother. He had no money, and she knew it. If the earlier enquiries about her hand had come to nothing, it is quite possible that a major reason was her father's lack of ability, or willingness, to put an acceptable offer on the table. Sir John was not the same kind of man as her father. He was more open-handed, but he was also even more broke. So there could yet be years when men and women who were casting about for wives for their sons and nephews sent out feelers to her family, and her family sent back half-hearted responses, and perhaps sometimes she even met up with the man, but the jointure agreement was never actually drawn up, the betrothal sealed.

Margery would not have wanted that. And perhaps if that pattern had set in, she would have been motivated to break it, even if she had to break with convention at the same time. But in reality that situation did not arise. Because she fell in love.

How it happened, when it happened, we shall never know. Margery and Richard were by nature, it seems, private and dignified people; this they kept to themselves, and rightly so. They had known each other a long time, though perhaps for much of it not all that well. For many years Richard was probably no more to her than a man of business who came to the house like many others, and paused sometimes to chat with her and the other children. She was to him one of those children: lively, pleasant looking, someone to whom he warmed, but not someone with whom he expected to be intimate. As she grew up, things changed, of course: they could talk, doubtless did talk, more equally. Crises came – her father's arrest, the attack on Hellesdon, her father's death – and perhaps (even probably, judging by what followed) he was someone to whom she turned. Opportunities came – London, not least – and perhaps they used them.

Barriers rose up. And they looked through them, walked past them.

It was surely not that they did so blindly. If he could at times be direct – sometimes too direct for those he dealt with – Richard was not an impetuous man, and certainly not a fool. He had no instinct for self-destruction; on the contrary, he seems to have been solidly motivated to make a success of his life. If he had sensed himself becoming fond of Margery, and realized that she was not, could never be for him, then he would surely have drawn back. If he did not draw back, it was probably because he believed that this was not true. Was he a suitable match for her? Most likely he asked himself that question, and the answer he came to was that he was.

Few men are given to underestimating their own attractions, and Richard was evidently not one of them. But he was far from being deluded in his conclusion, because from some perspectives at least, it was an entirely reasonable one. Compare the list of Richard's possessions abstracted from Hellesdon by the duke of Suffolk's men with the list of Sir John's possessions, and their owners look to be much the same kind of men. One side morrey gown, one side morrey gown; one book in French, one book in French. Compare the contents of Richard's money chest with the contents of Sir John's: well, Richard himself was probably the only person in a position to do that. The answer he came up with must have been comfortably in his own favour.

He must have been confident that he could provide for Margery in the way that she expected to be provided for. He had not inherited money, as far as we know, as most of the young men suggested for her had done, or expected to; but he had acquired money, a house, the ability to live the kind of life that people of the Berney, Mautby, (Norfolk-based) Paston class tended to live. He lived among people of that class, many of them had become his friends, and he can have perceived no insurmountable social barrier. He could make an intelligent guess at the kind of dowry that might be bestowed on her, and even if he might have wished for something more, he reckoned he could live with it. Anyway, by then he had fallen in love with her. This was not a match that he pursued because it was a wildly advantageous one; as far as we know he had never considered making a marriage primarily for money. There are no mentions in the papers of his that survive of rich widows who could have boosted his fortunes. Richard was in his way a desirable man, and if that kind of option had been his choice, he would have had little difficulty finding a woman to provide it. Evidently it never was.

He had served her father, and now he served her brother. Well, many men did that, and many of them were men whose wives drank ale and ate cakes with the Paston women. Richard cannot have seen it as a difficulty. That he was owed money by her brother was an awkwardness perhaps, but it was surely more awkward for Sir John than for him; if he could overlook it Sir John could too. He thought all this, most likely, in the days after he had first found himself talking with Margery in a new, a deeper, a different way; when he had found himself holding her eyes, and knowing that she was looking with just as much interest back at him. He did not see himself as asking her to ruin herself for him. Far from it: he had a good sense of what Margery wanted from life, and he was confident that he was the man to provide it for her.

Or so he told himself in his good moments. If we can imagine this much, we must also, in fairness, imagine another side. Because Margery did not confess to her mother or her brother that she was becoming very fond of Richard Calle. She did not so much as hint to them (as far as we can tell) that if they wanted to find her a husband, she would be grateful if they were to look in this direction. And Richard did not make an opportunity to stand by Sir John as they watched Margery – supervising the children at play, or chatting with friends on a Sunday after church – and mention to him that he was becoming remarkably

Church of St John the Baptist, Metfield, Suffolk

fond of the girl, fond enough that he would be happy to take her on, on terms that it would not prove difficult to agree. They could have – in retrospect, it is surely true that they should have – chosen to make it clear to their family and friends in what direction their thoughts and feelings were tending. And they did not.

So a part of them – of both of them, most likely – acknowledged that this was not what people expected of either of them. Of course there is a spectrum of responses that anyone makes when a friend or relation reveals an inclination; it is rarely a question of delight or fury, with nothing in between. Perhaps if Richard had told his brother John, say, that he was tempted to make an offer for the Paston girl, John would have said, are you sure? Attracts a lot of trouble, that family. Never much liked the father, and I wouldn't say young John III really regards me as a friend either. But if that is what you're set on, Richard, then of course I shall support you. And perhaps if Margery had confided in Anne – who was probably old enough by now to take an interest and have an opinion – then Anne would have been astonished she should be drawn by a man so much older than herself. And one with no interest in jousting at court, a country man, not one touched with glamour like their big brother. But if that's what you really want for yourself, Margery, then I wish you all the best.

Perhaps those were the confidences that the two of them did make first of all. But they probably did not make them until they had gone beyond the first barrier, and the second one too. (This does not imply that they became lovers in the physical sense; perhaps they did at this point, but perhaps not.) They did not make them at a time when they might have not just heard, but listened to the reservations in the answers they were given. They did not make them at a stage when they felt able to stand back a smidgen, and say to each other, perhaps, just perhaps, this is not wise of us.

No; they made them (if they made them at all) when it had gone further than that. There is much we do not know, but what we do know beyond reasonable doubt is that the choice Margery and Richard made was not one of logic. It was one of passion. And once the passion had caught them in its sweet grip, they were beyond listening to those reservations. They were beyond saying to each other, probably our friends and relations are right, and fond as we are of each other, we would be wiser if we were to look elsewhere.

They meant to have each other, whether others believed it was the right thing for them or not.

Church of
St John the Baptist,
Mileham, Norfolk

25
The best
chooser

One of his friends described Sir John Paston as 'the best chooser of a gentlewoman'[1] that he knew. An interesting choice of words, which leads to the questions: what did he mean by a gentlewoman, and what was Sir John choosing her for?

The context does not suggest a search for a wife, neither for himself nor for his friends. But a gentlewoman implies a woman of some standing: it is an unlikely synonym for a whore. Sir John was a flirt; we can take that as read. The shy lad who had failed to get established at court with only an introduction from a man unable or unwilling to push him in the right direction had long grown up, and now he was an established member of that court, not least because his wit and charm made him an asset to it. But the man who sired Constance did not always stop at flirting, and perhaps he did not usually stop there. Some at least of the gentlewomen he chose must have become his mistresses. There is a forlorn letter from one, Cecily Daune,[2] written around this time from Hellow in Lincolnshire. So Cecily was not playing at cards and dancing at Westminster: Sir John had either found her a good way away, or more likely he had packed her off a good way away. 'I have heard a report,' she wrote, with the careful but wounded politeness that is also apparent in Constance Reynforth's surviving letter, 'that you are going to be married to a daughter of the duke of Somerset.'

That was his uncle. But Sir John was on the lookout for a wife, and it was apparent that it was not to be Cecily Daune.

If Cecily had had his child, then the child did not survive, or (more likely) his mother never got to know about it. He had clearly stayed in contact with her. He was not a boor, though he seems to have been a bit of a cad. Probably his attempts to be fair to, or his genuine love for, women like Cecily and Constance played havoc with his attempts to marry. If he was lucky in love, he was not lucky in finding domestic bliss. When he settled on a suitable wife – he first made contact with the woman he chose around 1468, and they were betrothed by early 1469 – he made a choice that signally failed to work out. Anne Haute was a gentlewoman, doubtless considerably more affluent than Constance or Cecily, and better connected – she was a kinswoman of the queen, and had estates in west Norfolk. Sir John was head of the family, so he picked her for himself, she was not foisted on him. But after they had committed themselves (betrothal in those days was regarded as a binding contract, and not easily broken) they fell out so badly that the marriage itself never took place, and eventually Sir John went through the wearing and expensive business of extricating himself from the commitment.

The other gentlewomen might had had quite a lot to do with that.

Some of this was in the future when Richard and Margery first began to consider how they might best approach her family, but some of it was in the present and past. They both knew what Sir John was like. Quite likely they knew about the baby (or at least, one baby) he had sired. Richard must have heard John Daubeney's account of the goings-on at Caister – when Sir John was supposed to be showing contrition, and re-establishing his place in the family – that had so horrified Margaret. And he was travelling down to London and Westminster regularly and meeting up with Sir John, so he probably knew something about the current crop of gentlewomen too.

So Sir John was not a man unfamiliar with love, but he made a very clear distinction between that and marriage. He was also a man with social pretensions, and with a somewhat optimistic sense of the position his background and wealth enabled him and his family to claim. If he had talked to Margery of getting her married, he was quite likely talking about a grand marriage. He might well have scoffed at John Strange's nephew and his two hundred marks a year – nothing more was heard of that, and it is unlikely to have been entirely Margery's choice that it was so. The Pastons needed connections, from Sir John's perspective: ties to the upper classes that would make a reality of the claims in their fake genealogy. Perhaps they could not all do as brilliantly as Uncle William, but Margery was an attractive girl, with the great asset of Sir John as a brother (and the duke of Somerset's daughter as a future aunt). The man who had perhaps battled with his family over Constance, and had to swallow the loss and learn to look at such matters differently, was not likely to be wildly enthusiastic if his sister announced that she was not interested in being introduced to court, or even in another attempt to place her in Framlingham Castle, but had decided instead to marry the family's estate manager.

No point telling him that his hopes for her were hogwash if he did not have the money to put behind them. Margery and Richard decided instead to make their approach elsewhere.

It is perhaps surprising that they did not choose her mother. Margaret was no snob; on the contrary, she seems to have been one of the members of the family least comfortable with these new grand ambitions. There is no indication that she looked to appear at Westminster herself. What she wanted for the future, it was by now becoming apparent, was to retreat to Mautby, where she had clearly been happy in her girlhood, and live out her days in peace under the wide skies of south-east Norfolk. She would be near enough

to Caister to see much of her sons when they stayed there, but she was not looking to be allocated an apartment in the castle; the smaller, cosier, less pretentious house at Mautby was what she chose.

But if she did not want royal connections for herself, that does not mean she did not want them for her daughter. Anyway, although she would have had input, the decision was not hers to make.

Another reason for overlooking her might have lain in the wranglings that had followed John senior's death. At times Richard was probably faced with a hard choice of pleasing Margaret or pleasing her son, and he had evidently always chosen the son. How could he not, he might have thought? Sir John was his main master now, even if he continued to do some work for Margaret too. But it was never likely to endear him to Margaret. As well as the bitching about his closeness to William, there were probably other incidents, other times when Richard did not support Margaret in the way he had used to do when John senior was alive. Margaret was a resilient woman, but she was a resilient woman with a very good memory. She did not readily forgive such slights.

So they decided to begin with John III instead. John III was an affable man, and on good terms with them both, although he too had changed from the boy who was happy to help his mother in the counting house. The years at Framlingham and travelling with the duke of Norfolk, the fighting he had done for the king, the friendships he had made with knights and lords, must have widened his horizons, and his ambitions too.

John III was a realist, though, and not being the heir, he needed to be. He could not afford to base himself in London, and not just because his brother needed him in East Anglia, where he was playing a role not dissimilar to the one Margaret had played for his father. He seems to have stayed for much of the time at Caister. The main threats the Pastons still faced were in Suffolk, where Judge Yelverton and his supporters were continuing to dispute their title to many of the old Fastolf lands, and from Caister it was relatively easy for him to ride over to Cotton or any other place where it was necessary to counter what Yelverton and Jenney did, and to remind the tenants what the Pastons looked like.

John III was not averse to the courtly pursuits he had practised in his Framlingham days, though. Jousting was one of his passions, and his brother helped to ensure that he still had the opportunity sometimes to indulge it.

Margery would not have been living with her brother; she was kept at her mother's side. Although the women would have seen a fair amount of him when they were at Mautby, they were probably not as close now as they had been a few years earlier. John III must have seen her and Richard together from time to time, but if he had noticed that things between them had changed, he had said nothing to either of them about it.

Church of St Peter Hungate, Norwich

Would he be supportive? They did not know.

So they decided not to approach John III directly, but to sound him out obliquely. A sense of how he viewed the possibility would be enough for a start. Then they could fix on their next step: to be more frank with him and ask for his support, or to speak to Sir John, Margaret or even William.

The intermediary they chose was a man called Lovell.[3] He must have been a friend of Richard's, and a gentleman of some means. One reason for picking him was that Lovell had a son who was looking to marry. This could be his excuse for talking to John III: that he wanted to know how things lay with Margery, whether she was committed to a suitor, or whether new approaches might be made for her hand.

Entrusting a task like this to another man is no easy thing. Richard and Margery must both have had an apprehensive time as they waited for Lovell to find an opportunity to talk to John III, and to come back to them with a report.

Perhaps they heard first from John III himself, although if he said anything he said it to his sister (or to his mother, who would have repeated it to his sister), because he swore afterwards that he had never discussed the issue with Richard Calle. The reason was

Norwich

obvious: he was not just ambivalent about the possibility of Richard marrying Margery, he was dead set against it. He probably believed that once he had made his feelings clear (he guessed that Lovell would report back, so even if he himself did not have words with Margery, the lovers would learn what he thought), the idea would be dead. He had to work with Richard, so the least said the better if the man took a while to put his hopes behind him.

Lovell told Richard what was said by the two of them, though he would have glossed over the moments when he fumbled for words, and made excuses if he had taken an approach that was different from the one Richard had suggested to him. (The conversation degenerated into a quarrel at the end, and he might have missed out that bit too.) He had asked John III at the outset how things stood between Margery and Richard, which was maybe not what Richard had intended. For all he had said nothing to either of them, John III, did not seem surprised at the possibility of an involvement. His response had foxed Lovell, though: did Calle put you up to this, he wanted to know?

Lovell hummed and hawed, and it was a while before he remembered what he was supposed to say, particularly as John III became quite aggressive, and refused to take his equivocation for an answer. He did not deny it even then – one problem with this intermediary, evidently, was that he was a painfully honest man – but only settled for not confirming it. The enquiry was prompted by his son most of all, he claimed. But then he seems to have realized belatedly that he was not actually interested in putting forward his son as a suitor, so he hastily added that it was his son enquiring on behalf of a friend.

John III would scarcely have swallowed that old ruse. And he cannot have reckoned much to Lovell's son as a marriage prospect either, since he declined to be sidestepped and went back to basics. What this is really about, he said bluntly, is Calle and my sister, isn't it? And let me be plain, since I want to see a stop put to it. Even if my mother said yes to it; if Sir John was willing to let it happen; if my father was not dead and he had agreed – not, mind you, that any of that is feasible – I still would never agree to Richard Calle taking my sister off to sell candles and mustard in Framlingham.

So the first misstep that led to a war was Margery and Richard's, but the second was John III's. This was a moment when things might have taken a peaceable turn, but they did not.

Candles and mustard. It must have struck Richard as downright offensive. Not that there was any shame in running a successful grocer's shop, and even less when you compared it with some of the things the Pastons had done. But John III had deliberately picked not on what he was now, but on where he had come from. He must have plucked that analogy out of the air – the knight in the castle at the top of the hill, the cringing servant behind his counter at the foot – but it was a crude and nasty way of emphasizing the differences between the two families. Perhaps if John III had taken Richard aside, and told him, in confidence, that he was fairly sure he had found a splendid match for his sister; that he knew Richard had become very fond of her, and would take it as a personal favour if he chose not to stand in the way – perhaps (but only perhaps) he would have chosen to back off.

There was no way he was backing off now.

26
Such
good
cheer

It was out in the open now. And at some point, whether it followed fast on John III's conversation with Lovell, or came a few weeks later when Sir John was next at Caister, words must have been had with Margery.

The details are lost, but logic says that initially they would have been kind words: or kind, at least, once her mother had made sure she was not pregnant. So much on their minds: it was understandable that getting Margery married had not had the attention it might have had. But this had brought them up short, and made it clear it was high time. So she could expect now that new feelers would be put out, and that those put in would be caught and explored. If she had been fretting that there was no provision for a dowry, well, she need fret no more: some money or land would be found, even if her grandmother had to be leaned upon to provide it. What more natural than that she should want to marry? Her family wanted this for her too, and they would make it a priority now to ensure that it happened.

It was not only Richard who knew how to be stubborn. Thank you, Margery must have said, but I have chosen the man I wish to wed. All that is needed is for you to give us your blessing.

John III was not mistaken, though. It was not only he who did not want this. Agnes Paston, Margaret Paston, Sir John Paston, William Paston and his aristocratic bride: none of them were happy at the prospect of Margery's becoming Mistress Calle.

Fine hands though the Pastons were at brewing feuds, nobody wanted the question of Margery's marriage to become one: not Margery, not her family, and certainly not Richard, who was dependent on the family for the bulk of his work. So when Margery was urged to wait for a while, to meet with some young men, to consider very carefully whether she had made the right choice, she can have had little option but to agree. Richard might not have liked it, but he had to acquiesce too. And for some time – months, perhaps half a year – this must have been done. Young lads like Strange's nephew were invited to Caister, or meetings set up at Princes Inn. Margery was chaperoned now, especially but not only when Richard was close at hand, and her family watched to see if one of these heaps of kindling might catch fire.

Sometimes it happens; sometimes any conceivable thing happens. But it does not happen often when two people are at that stage when the sky seems greyer if the one they love is not in sight. Margaret and her sons might have believed they were making headway, and that when they pressed her, Margery was sure to pick one of these approved young suitors. But Margery probably believed that this was simply a waiting period she was forced to endure before she got what she had chosen.

The summer of 1468 was a wedding season, but it was not a family wedding that occupied the Paston family. Instead it was a royal wedding. The king's sister, Margaret of York, was making a brilliant marriage to the duke of Burgundy, one of the richest nobles in Europe, and Sir John Paston and his brother were invited by the king and his sister to join the retinue that would take her to Bruges for the ceremony.[1]

How could they refuse? Very easily, their creditors might have muttered, particularly because this was an honour that they would have to fund themselves, the king also being somewhat short of ready cash. But just as it must have seemed unimaginable to Margery that she would not get the man of her choice, so it was beyond the comprehension of the Paston brothers that any sane man would not be thrilled to escort the king's sister to a foreign court.

Nor was it a disappointment. John III wrote breathlessly back to his mother about the processions, the pageants, and especially the jousting. 'There were never Englishmen had so good cheer out of England that ever I heard of,' he summarized his own and his brother's opinion. The only disappointment was that the festivities had to be wrapped up more speedily than had been intended, because the news had come that the king of France, who was threatening war with Burgundy, was heading rapidly for Bruges and was by then less than five days' journey away.

That is what happens all too often when men distract themselves with festivities: their enemies creep up while they are not looking. And John III (who, decent man as he generally was, also sent his best wishes to his sisters and the rest of the household, though he did not send them to Richard Calle) perhaps knew that this piece of extravagance was in many ways more than he and his brother could afford.

It was coincidence perhaps that it was about this time that the happy honeymoon that Sir John Paston and his family had enjoyed when he took over as its head came to an end. Or perhaps it was not entirely a coincidence. Although many of the legal details are lost to us, common sense says that one reason was the familiar one of promises not fulfilled and debts not paid. William Worcester had not yet been granted his little house at Drayton. He cannot have been the only, or the most important, of the men who felt they had been let down. And if those creditors enquired where Sir John was, or John III, and got the answer, off on a jaunt with Princess Margaret, it would not have improved their inclination to wait a while longer. It had been two years now since John senior died, long enough for Sir John to bed into his role and to get his affairs into some kind of order. Men were getting a sense now that it would probably never be done.

Judge Yelverton's continuing enmity was bad enough, but they could have coped, most likely, if it stayed at that. The ravaged house and fields at Cotton could be quietly forgotten, while the estate servants focused on collecting the rent and harvesting the crops in less contentious places. Things took a much more serious turn, though, when a smaller man and a greater both slid over to the side of the Pastons' enemies.

The small man was Thomas Howes, Fastolf's old secretary, who had retained his place as joint executor of the will with John senior, and then with his son.[2] His recollection of the events of the days before Fastolf's death had always been crucial, and whoever else he chose to overlook, John senior seems always to have done as much as was necessary to keep Howes on board. Probably there was a genuine warm feeling between the two men, of the kind that intensifies under pressure. There was no such warm feeling between Howes and Sir John Paston. Whatever had been done under his father was evidently being done no longer. Howes was not happy, and in time he chose to talk to Judge Yelverton and his cronies about his unhappiness, and more.

The greater man was the duke of Norfolk.

Here too the details are sketchy, the conversations and writs long lost, so we can only guess at the precise reasons for Norfolk's change of allegiance, and point to the obvious underlying factors, the long-established pressure points. It hardly seems sufficient cause that John III had left Framlingham and based himself at Caister; any man could have understood his reasons for doing that. The Pastons' failure fully to observe the duke's instructions at Cotton might have had some influence. To suggest that the duke took offence on Richard Calle's behalf is a stretch, though he probably heard of both Richard's ambitions and John III's opinion of them, and being less of a snob than some of his courtiers, thought it a shabby way to treat the man.

Norfolk coveted Caister just as his father had. He had grown now into his high position, acquired the power to face down men that he had not had years back when William Jenney ignored his commands. And there were presumably other matters he heard of, other quarrels that had had damp earth tipped over them in the weeks after John senior's funeral, where the weeds had now pushed to the surface. They built to a sufficient size that when Judge Yelverton, William Jenney and their friends made an approach to him, he chose to listen to it.[3]

The deal he apparently came to with them involved Howes, as executor of Fastolf's will, and Yelverton, Jenney and other men who could claim, with Howes's support, to be acting as trustees of the estate. In that capacity they had sold Cotton to the claimant who vandalized its manor. Now, in that same capacity, they sold Caister Castle to the duke of Norfolk.

Church of St Michael, Oxnead, Norfolk

27
The
blazing
star

A little before Michaelmas 1468, in the damp days of approaching winter, a blazing
star appeared in the sky. For five or six weeks it made its inexorable way across the
heavens, from west to north, dragging a trail men reckoned to be four feet high. Sights
such as this have always been reckoned as portents of great upheavals, dramatic events.
These were weeks when many people glanced warily up at the comet and its glittering tail,
and wondered what fortunes it was bringing with it.[1]

Margery Paston and Richard Calle were of course among them.

They must have done as Margery's family required over the previous months: he had
waited patiently, she had dutifully met with other suitors. There was no point in that
charade continuing for longer, even if it was not fast becoming impossible in the face of
the new threats to the estates. Neither Sir John nor any of his family could afford to put
time into hunting down still more eligible young men, discussing terms in outline with
their guardians, setting up chaperoned meetings, and exchanging letters afterwards, which
had to be phrased with increasing care as it became evident each time that Margery would
not agree to the match. Now it was time to push forward their own agenda.

Margery must have pleaded to be allowed her choice. He might not be what her family
wanted for her, but surely Richard would not make so intolerable a relative? Surely they
valued his loyalty over the long and often difficult years when he had served the family;

surely they needed his knowledge and his support? Richard too must have approached Sir John, and made it clear that he had a long-standing attachment to his sister, and would like to marry her. Even if he had to make his case to the man's back, he would still have done his best to spell out the terms of his offer.

Why did Sir John refuse?

From today's perspective it is difficult, even impossible to understand. Richard does not seem to us a particularly inadequate suitor. True, this would not have been a brilliant marriage for Margery, but nor would it been a disgraceful one. Compared with, say, her becoming pregnant by a man who then disowned her, or running off to join the gypsies, it was a creditable outcome. And as well as the prospects for Margery, the Pastons surely had to consider the implications of estranging Richard. He knew tales that dead men as well as living ones had told him. He and his family had long been a crucial conduit to Framlingham Castle, and this was no small consideration in the circumstances. And however carefully they had tried to shut him out of their more questionable dealings, still he must have had more than enough information that Judge Yelverton, say, would have been delighted to obtain. This was a threat they could have neutralized immediately by bringing Richard into the family. By angering him, they intensified it.

There were probably reasons that have left no trace. Perhaps the kinds of words had been exchanged that cannot readily, if ever, be forgiven. Perhaps things had been done, of the kind that any family, even the most diligent with its papers, keeps well clear of the historical record, which made the Paston men (though not Richard) convinced the match was impossible. Perhaps there was a depth of bitterness in Sir John, and for all we know in his brother too, that they had been forbidden to follow their hearts, and were damned if they would let Margery do what had not been allowed them. Perhaps we cannot fully fathom the intensity of their determination to resist any threat, however marginal, to their social position. They might have been declared gentle-born by no less than the king, but many people must still have believed that the truth was quite different.

Perhaps it was no more than that a family which had clung so often to impossible positions simply did not know to reverse its cart out of this narrow alley. Margery's mother and her brothers had all said no; it was not in their family lexicon to think again, and tell her yes.

So there was a time when Margery and Richard hoped for permission, and then there must have been the steadily deepening realization that there was no prospect of their

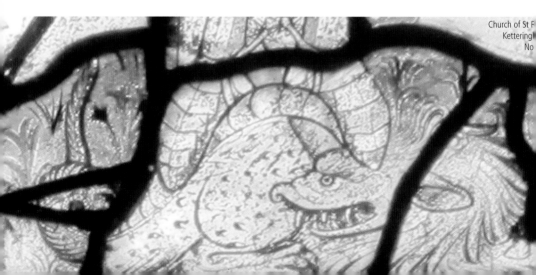

Church of St F
Kettering
No

obtaining it. It might be irrational, self-defeating, cruel, but this was the line her family had taken.

They could submit, accept the 'no' that had been given, and choose both of them to look elsewhere. Margery's mother, her grandmother, perhaps her aunt too, and other old friends of the family doubtless pleaded with her to do so. You might feel passion now, they could have told her, but such blazing stars do not last for ever. They disappear from your sky like the comet. In time every man and woman looks on those they once loved to distraction, and wonders what the appeal of them can ever have been.

Richard's friends probably did the same with him. She's pretty enough, bright and lively: but put another girl in your bed, and you'll soon forget that one.

But Margery was a Paston. She was no more given to backing down than the rest of her family. And though Richard remained loyal, in spite of what must at times have been much temptation to turn his coat, he too was stubborn. That his suit was denied must have bitten deep. He could not bring himself to accept it.

If they did not submit, they would have to fight. The fight would probably be a long and hard one, and there could be no certainty that they would win it. They surely knew that, and they decided that it was what they would do.

Margery and Richard were not the only ones making preparations for a fight at this time. Sir John and John III were working on their defence of the Fastolf lands.

There was of course a legal side to this: although John senior was long gone, the family was far from short of lawyers, and just as the Paston way was to dig their heels in firmly when they encountered opposition, so it was to send off a hailstorm of writs. But there was more. If it was necessary, they would defend Caister by force. It was a strong castle, but still it needed men to stand on its battlements, to aim their crossbows out of the window slits. That November Sir John set about enlisting them. This was not the kind of force that he had put together at Hellesdon, since however he shuffled his funds he could not have found the money for that. But he hired 'four trustworthy and true men'.[2] John III would head the garrison, and the estate servant who had come to the fore in the previous few years, John Daubeney, would stand by his side and give him advice. All the men were trained soldiers, capable and willing if necessary to use a gun or a crossbow. 'They are sad and sensible men,' Sir John wrote to his brother, except for a bald man called William Penny, who he had to admit was a known drunkard. 'But he is no brawler', he added hopefully. If this seemed less than the circumstances demanded, it was the best he could do.

What the lovers should do by way of preparation for their battle, it was probably Richard who decided. He would have suggested it only when Margery assured him that she was willing – no, determined – to endure whatever her family did to her, and to force them to accept him as her husband. By this time Margery must have been kept under close watch whenever Richard visited Caister, or Mautby, or whichever of the family's houses she was staying at. But she could not be watched every moment of every day. The pair had friends and well-wishers, even more so as it became apparent how much opposition they faced. Margery's sister Anne was probably one of them. They could (and did) write to each other. And they clearly found at least one opportunity to be alone together. They used it well.

In an era when men could force through a testacy based on an unwritten will, there was both looseness and tightness in what it took to bind a couple to each other. Loose, in the sense that although they were usual, witnesses to the commitment were not essential. If a couple spoke the right words to each other, made the right promises, it was as binding as a marriage blessed by the parson at the church gate. Tight, in the sense that if both parties affirmed that this had been done, it was all but impossible for anyone subsequently to tear them apart.

Sir John was to find to his cost, in the years ahead, just how binding a betrothal could be. Margery and Richard were to prove that too, but in their case the commitment was something they not only wanted when they made it, but continued to want in the months and years that followed.

Where and when they did this, we do not know. We do not even know what form of words they used, since this too has become fogged by the centuries that separate us from them. But we know that it was done at around this time. They found a place that was as suitable as they could contrive it – a church porch for choice, an attic if that was the best they could do. There they took each other's hands, held each other's gaze fast, and each in turn said the words that bound them together. I promise to take you as my wife; I promise to take you as my husband. If they had a witness they kept quiet about it afterwards, so more likely they did not. They probably exchanged tokens: a ring was usual, as it is now. A kiss, or depending on how private was the place they had met, something more. Now we are bound, they agreed with each other, as securely as if the bishop had married us.

Then Margery headed home and told her mother and her brothers, and the storm broke out around them.

From a 'seven sacraments' font in All Saints Church, Gresham, Norfolk

28
Let run
the waters

Norwich

What her family did to Margery we again must mostly guess. What happened to Elizabeth a couple of decades before is probably a good template. She must have been beaten: sometimes thrashed systematically, sometimes caught by her mother's or grandmother's swiftly lashing arm. Just as Elizabeth had, she probably had to stay close at home sometimes for fear others would notice the scabs, the black eyes, the scrapes on her hands where she had put her arms up to defend herself.

She was harangued, of course, by all of them: not just her mother, her grandmother, her brothers and uncles, but Father Gloys too. And threatened most likely with other punishments: being locked in the dark in the cellar, being deprived of her supper. Then there would be times when they tried to haul her to shore with kindness, promising that they would listen, bring friends to speak with her, offering her hope.

She swore still that she had tied herself to Richard Calle.

Her family sent Anne away, to board with another family, perhaps largely so that she could not help the lovers to get messages to each other. They thought of sending Margery too: her mother suggested Lady Oxford or Lady Bedford,[1] the mistresses of imposing households where the chamberlain kept the door tight closed and Margery would not only be distracted, she would also be pinned up well away from Richard. This would be a good idea since 'we be either of us weary of each other',[2] her mother wrote to Sir John. She meant more than she chose to put on the page, because she added that she would expand on this when she next saw him.

Months went by. It seems that Margery was not sent away, perhaps because there was no money to pay Lady Oxford or Lady Bedford. She must have been made to spend hours with Father Gloys, ordered to pray on her knees that she might see sense and obey her family. She told him too, perhaps, that she had made a binding commitment to Richard Calle. We'll see about that, was probably his answer. Tell me the words you used, and I'll tell you whether they were as binding as you claim.

She was not falling for a ruse as simple as that one. Father Gloys was her mother's tool. I'll tell them to the bishop, she might have answered him. He'll listen to me, and perhaps believe.

What happened on the Pastons' lands meanwhile, we know rather better. Judge Yelverton and his son demanded rents, in Suffolk and in Norfolk too. They rode about the land 'with spears and lances like men of war',[3] trying to disrupt the ploughing in that spring of 1469, or even frighten those who did not support them sufficiently that they would abandon their farms.

The duke of Norfolk's men were also active in Norfolk as well as Suffolk. They targeted Hainford, an estate that had been Fastolf's just north of Norwich. They felled trees there and carted off the wood. They even drained some of the stewponds, and achieved what the duke of Suffolk had not: they managed to steal the Pastons' fish.[4]

At Caister, John III's little garrison practised their archery, and perhaps saw some action against the duke of Norfolk's men, come to stake their master's claim to the castle. Whether in earnest or in sport, they worked hard enough that they broke three or four steel bows, including Sir John's, John Pamping's and one belonging to Robert Jackson, one of the hired-in men. John III wrote to his brother in London, to see if he could find a man to mend them.[5]

All these months, Richard continued to work for the Pastons. His relations with John III seem to have been close to breaking point (when Sir John told his brother to get money off Richard, he got a sharp answer back that 'God help me I will none ask him'[6]), but he was getting on well enough, it seems, with Sir John. He did not practise archery with the Caister garrison, or learn from bald William Penny how to load and fire a gun, and this was perhaps also part of the reason for John III's coldness. The Calles supported the dukes of Norfolk, always had, always would. Richard would do much for the Paston family, but aiming an arrow from a steel bow at the duke's liveried men was not among the much that he would do.

Chapel of St Nicholas, Gipping, Suffolk

That April or so Richard was down in London, dealing with Sir John, William Paston and the other men he usually met with there. He wrote to Sir John a short while later, when he was back at Caister.[7] He had borrowed a hundred shillings from Margaret, as he had been ordered to do 'for Mariot's matter', but he had managed to repay two-thirds of it. (He must have made a priority of this: annoying Margaret was definitely not his intention.) He had gone over the household bills with John Daubeney, and handed him thirty shillings. Since he had received only eighteen shillings and tenpence from Sir John since he returned from London, a good twelve shillings of this had come from elsewhere: he had borrowed from some other men, but had had no luck when he tried to get money out of William Paston. Although the price of malt was a feeble twenty pence a quarter, he reckoned there was no better option than to sell the stock, because the men were complaining grievously that they had not had their wages, and something would have to be done about that.

Richard had not had his own wages either. They were a year behind at this point.

Finally, he added, Robert Jackson's crossbow was broken. Should he send it to London to be mended? That shows how much he had liaised with John III.

Church of St John the Baptist, Mileham, Norfolk

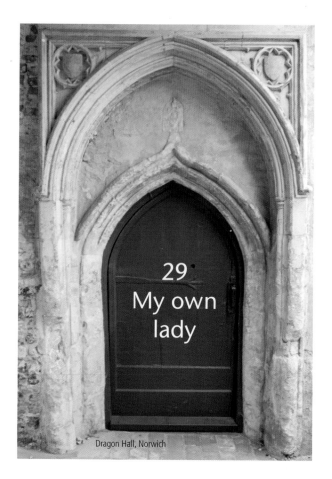

29
My own
lady

Dragon Hall, Norwich

Getting a message to Margery was hard, but Richard tried. He wrote her a long letter some time in 1469. Perhaps it was one of many. This one must have been intercepted, because it ended up among the family's papers, so possibly Margery never got to read it.

My own lady and mistress and before God very true wife, I with full sorrowful heart recommend me to you, as one that cannot be merry nor shall be, till it be otherwise with us than it is yet; for this life that we lead now is no pleasure to God nor to the world, considering the great bond of matrimony that is made between us and also the great love that has been and, as I trust, is yet between us, and on my part never greater. Wherefore I beseech Almighty God to comfort us as soon as it pleases Him, for we that ought by right to be most together are most asunder. It seems to me a thousand years ago since I spoke with you. I had rather than all the goods in the world that I might be with you. Alas, alas! good lady, those that keep us asunder remember full little what they do. Four times a year are those cursed that hinder matrimony. It makes many men to think they have other things on their conscience as well. But what, lady, suffer as you have to and make merry as you can, for I know, lady, that in the long term God will of his righteousness help his servants that mean truly and would love each other according to his laws.

I understand, lady, you have had as much sorrow for me as any gentlewoman has had in the world. I would to God all that sorrow that you have had rested on me so that you could be discharged of it, for it is like death to me that you are treated otherwise than you ought to be.

Church of St Mary, Shelton, Norfolk

This is a painful life we lead; I cannot live thus without it being a great displeasure to God.

You should know that I had sent you a letter from London by my lad, and he told me he could not speak with you, as there was so careful watch kept over both him and you. He told me John Thresher came to him in your name and said that you sent him to my lad for a letter or token that I should have sent you, commanding him to deliver it to him, but my lad did not trust him, so he gave him nothing. Afterwards he brought him a ring, saying that you sent it to him, commanding him again to deliver the letter or token, but my lad and I reckoned that it was not your doing, it was done by my mistress and Sir James [Gloys].

Alas, what do they mean? I suppose that they think we are not contracted together, and if they do I marvel, for they are not well advised, remembering how plainly I spoke to my mistress at the beginning and I suppose you did so too, if you did as you ought rightly to have done. If you did the contrary, as I have been informed, you did not speak according to conscience nor to the pleasure of God, unless you did it for fear and to please those who were at that time about you; and if you did it for this reason it was a reasonable cause, considering the great and importunate pressure upon you and that you were told many an untrue tale about me, which, God knows, I was never guilty of.

My lad told me that my mistress your mother asked him if he had brought any letter to you, and she said a lot more, and among the rest, at the last she said to him that I would not make her privy to the beginning but she supposed I would at the end. And as to that, God knows she knew it first of me and no other. I do not know what she meant, for by my truth there is no gentlewoman alive that my heart is more tender to than her, or is more reluctant to displease, except only yourself, whom of very right I ought to feel tender to and love the best, for I am bound to you by the law of God, and so will do while I live, whatever becomes of it.

I suppose if you tell them sadly the truth they will not damn their souls for you. If I tell them the truth they will not believe me as well as they will do you. And therefore, good lady, at the reverence of God be plain to them and tell the truth, and if they will in no way agree to it, then let it be between God, the devil and them. The peril that we should be in, I beseech God should lie upon them and not on us. I am heavy and sorry to remember their disposition. God send them grace to guide all things well, as well as I wish they did. God be their guide and send them peace and rest.

I marvel much that they should take this matter so heavily as I understand they do, remembering that it is in such a case as cannot be remedied, and my deserts are such that it is thought there should be no obstacle against it. And also, the worship to them is not in your marriage but in their own marriage, which I beseech God send them one that may be to their worship and pleasure to God and to their heart's ease, for else it were a great pity.

Mistress, I am afraid to write to you, for I understand you have showed them my letters that I have sent you before this time, but I pray you let no creature see this letter. As soon as you have read it let it be burned, for I wish no one else to see it. …

Almighty Jesus preserve, keep, and give you your heart's desire, which I believe shall well be to God's pleasure. This letter was written with as great pain as I ever wrote anything in my life, for in good faith I have been right sick, and yet am not verily well at ease. God amend it, etc.

Church of St Mary, Martham, Norfolk

30 Bound more surely

Ethelbert Gate,
Norwich Cathedral

She was committed to Richard, she had told her family so many times over, and still they refused to accept it. What to do now to persuade them? Because if they were persuaded, Margery must have believed, they would have no option but to accept the betrothal as binding, and to allow the pair of them to marry.

Perhaps the bishop of Norwich could help her.

Father Gloys might have mentioned the bishop, or a friend, or perhaps Margery had gone to the cathedral with her mother when they were in Norwich, and looked on him as he conducted the service, and thought to herself, I could ask him. And the more she thought, the better an idea it must have seemed to her.

The advantage of the bishop was, men listened to him and respected him. Walter Lyhert had held the bishopric of Norwich for all of Margery's lifetime and more, and he wielded much power and influence in the city and beyond it. Some bishops kept to the church and cloister, serving God but not man, but Lyhert had never been one of those. He was a man who intervened even when many believed he should not. True, his interventions so far had been so little to the Pastons' taste that they had generally refused his offers to mediate, but even if Margery knew of that she had no reason to take it as her pattern. This was no dispute over land; betrothal and marriage were holy sacraments. If you trusted anyone, you had to trust bishops and priests to fear God enough that they did what was right in matters of faith and religion. She was sure she and Richard had said the right words, and said them in the right way. Now she needed a man with the knowledge to confirm that judgement, and with clout to make sure it was acted upon.

Father Gloys was not a viable substitute. First, he was firmly on the side of her mother, and second, he had minimal influence with her brothers. He would probably persuade himself that she had not committed herself whatever she told him, and even if he confirmed that the betrothal was binding, he could not have made her family accept it. It had to be the bishop.

Bishop Lyhert was a great man in many ways, but he had not achieved his high position by being any kind of holy fool. Even men who reckoned that when he mediated he was better than most in listening to the arguments of both sides acknowledged that he hesitated to give any verdict that angered powerful men. Perhaps Margery did not fully appreciate the extent to which the bishop's famous interventions served the bishop's own interests. When he could see no advantage in mediating, the bishop did not offer to mediate.

And when the bishop was first asked – not by Margery's family, so either by Margery herself, or by Richard, or conceivably by Father Gloys or another friend or colleague – if he would please intervene in this matter, the bishop did nothing.[1]

They had to ask him many times over. Many people eventually had a hand in asking him. And when the bishop finally indicated that he had listened to the pleas, and would indeed hear the case and give his verdict, Margery's mother and grandmother set to work. They embarked on a delaying campaign.

For a while this worked, but not for long. It did not amuse the bishop when he sent for Margery to appear before him and she did not come. Once he realized it was her mother who was behind the girl's failure to appear, he sent for Margaret. She took Agnes Paston along with her to the bishop's palace (perhaps Agnes had been sent for too), and they did their best to excuse the delays.

If they argued that from the family's perspective the timing was bad, it was because this was all too true. It was now September of 1469. A week or two earlier the duke of Norfolk's men had advanced on Caister in earnest. To have their homes attacked was a familiar matter, of course, to the Pastons, but they had never faced a threat like this one before. Caister was a real castle, not a manor house with a few light fortifications. It was much too strong to be taken in an afternoon, like Gresham or Hellesdon. It was designed for defence, and the Paston brothers had chosen to defend it. John III, John Daubeney and their little troop of men – augmented slightly from those Sir John had hired the year before, but not by much – were pinned in the castle, with the duke of Norfolk's

men conducting a siege from the water meadows. These men were not wielding staves and pitchforks, they had crossbows and cannon. There were a great many of them, both trained troops and tenants who had moseyed over to Caister to show their support for the duke. In short, the Pastons were at war.

No reason, the bishop reckoned, to cause a delay.

But the men of the family needed to, had to appear, or so Margaret and Agnes argued. Sir John was head of the family; he ought to be there. William Paston was one of Margery's father's executors, so he had a legitimate interest too. Could they not wait until it was possible for these men to come up to Norwich?

No, they could not.

Well, said Margaret, I shall not bring her to be examined, and nor shall I allow her to bring herself.

If he had been a Paston, the bishop and Margaret might well have had an argument then that Norwich would never have heard the last of, but Bishop Lyhert was a different kind of man. He said kindly enough to Margaret that he well understood what a trial her daughter was proving to her. For Margaret's sake, for Agnes's, for the sake of all her family and friends, he wished it had not come to this. He would like such a difficulty in his own family no better than she liked it in hers. But now it had come to it, and there was no dodging that hard fact. The matter had to be resolved, and since he had been requested so earnestly and so often to resolve it, he meant to examine the girl, and Richard too, and see what they said, then give a verdict that he would require all of them on their Christian conscience to accept.

Margaret gave it one last try. Before you ask her what she said to Calle, she begged him, make her understand what her answer will mean. And bear in mind too, please, that her grandmother and I have had many words with her about this, and both of us are right convinced that nothing the pair can have said to each other has bound them firmly. We both believe Margery is free to make another choice. Remind her, please, that that is what all of her family and friends wish her to do. Remind her what misery she will face if she defies us, because it has got to a pitch now where her family will never have anything more to do with her if she persists in marrying him.

Bishop Lyhert listened, and he promised. But he was no walkover: he would not let Margery's mother or her grandmother be with her, he said, when the girl gave her testimony.

Once in motion, the bishop wasted no time. The following day – a Friday – Margery was sent for to appear in front of him.

The Guildhall, Norwich

Chapel of St Nicholas, Gipping, Suffolk

Much as she had wanted this, it must have been downright terrifying. A man called Ashfield, an associate of the Pastons, came to Princes Inn (or whichever of the Pastons' houses she was then living at) to collect her, probably with an escort of a couple of servants. He made no secret of the fact that he sympathized with her family, and hoped the bishop would take the opportunity to shove her firmly back into line. Many people in Norwich knew by now of the dispute, and it must have been the gossip of the city that it was being put to the bishop. There would have been plenty of curious glances as the pair walked down Elm Hill and across Tombland. The sharp high spire of Norwich Cathedral loomed over them. They went through one of the great gates that punctuated the precinct walls, rounded the church and cloisters, and knocked on the door of the bishop's palace, where the bishop's servants were waiting to admit them.[2]

It was a relief to her, surely, that she did not have to do it in front of her mother and grandmother, who would have glared at her throughout, and might well have hissed and called out if she said the wrong thing. But she had perhaps not realized until she was brought into the bishop's chamber that neither would the examination be private. Ashfield stayed in the room throughout, and so did other people. These would have included servants of the bishop, and a clerk to make a note of what was said. There were probably other men there too, invited to witness this formal examination. Such things did not take place often, so plenty of people were eager to enjoy the day's entertainment at first hand, and regale their friends with accounts of it afterwards.

Margery probably guessed – and she was correct – that as soon as the questioning was over, her mother would be asking round to find out who had been there. Then she would track each man down, and question them minutely about everything that had been said.

A bishop was a lord of the land. He expected, and received, the deference of men and women much greater than Margery. She would have knelt, kissed his hand, and perhaps was left to stay on her knees as the bishop began to speak.

He kept his word to her mother, so first she was given a good long sermon. The importance of family was his first subject. Her father, her grandfather, her eldest brother at court: she should remember the value of her kin. And she should consider well not just the place of her family in society, but the importance of their good will to her, Margery Paston. She should think on her friends (he perhaps nodded at Ashfield), on the importance of friendship, and not least, on the significant fact that anyone might well lose their friends if they did things that those friends were not happy about. Her kin, of course, would remain her kin whatever she did; but, the bishop pointed out, her kin had made it more than plain to him that they would not tolerate it if she chose a husband they could not accept. She might well find herself denied their doors and disinherited. She should think hard on what this would mean for her.

He had heard, said the bishop, that Margery had come to love a man whom her family and friends were not content to see as her husband. He explained the purpose of this examination: that he wished to know what she had said to this man, and he to her. A betrothal was a solemn act, and as she knew, a binding one. If she had indeed committed herself, the church would not deny the commitment. But she should think carefully about what she had said, and what her family and friends wished she had said. She should consider how she related the tale now. For if he was persuaded that she and Richard Calle were committed to each other, then he would have no option but to pronounce that they should proceed to marry. And her life would change at that point, taking her down a path from which there was no return.

I understand that, said Margery. I shall tell you the truth.

He asked her then what she and Richard had said and done. And she told him, as fully and honestly as she could. The handfast, the tokens, the words: these were what men and women of their time understood as a betrothal. Richard had rehearsed with her the words that they would say before they carried out their private ceremony. She must have replayed it in her mind many times since, in the dead months when her mother had been trying to wear her down. She remembered exactly what he had said to her, and she to him.

And is it your understanding, asked Bishop Lyhert, that these exchanges added up to a binding betrothal?

It was. But she wanted to be surer of it than that. So she lifted her eyes up to the bishop's, in front of Master Ashfield, the servants and the rest, and asked if she might say something more.

She might if she wished, the bishop conceded.

Then let me tell you this, said Margery. As best as I know and understand, what Richard Calle and I said to each other bound us together. That is what I meant it to be, and what he meant too. In conscience we are committed, as we both chose to be. But if you judge, sir, that the words were not enough, then tell me so I can make

Church of St Mary, Saxlingham Nethergate, Norfolk

them right. If you need it to be surer, then tell me what I must say now, so I can make it as tight as it can be before I go from here.

The bishop did not ask her to say more, and she maybe regretted that. Though not an unkind man, his attitude probably struck her as forbidding, and she might have been far from sure that she had done what was needed. But she could be confident that she had done her best.

All this said, she was led out of the bishop's chamber. Ashfield left – as Margery most likely assumed, to do as he had been ordered, and report straight back to Margaret and Agnes Paston. Perhaps she glimpsed Richard briefly as he too headed in to speak with the bishop. Then she waited, with the Paston servants and the bishop's attendants, for the bishop to summon her back in and give his verdict.

It might not have been a long wait, because when she was led back to the chamber it was to be told that the bishop was not ready to pronounce. Richard probably asked, is there any difference then between what you were told by Mistress Margery and by me? Even if he did not say so in so many words, they would have known by the bishop's response that there was not. It was not this that was the problem.

The problem was that if this was what they both chose, it was certainly not what the bishop wanted them to choose. He had given them every chance to pull back, he had made it clear what price they would pay if they did not do so, and what he had hoped for was sufficient difference in their stories, or sufficient deficiency in what they had said and done, that he could with a clear conscience pronounce that the betrothal was not

Dragon Hall, Norwich

binding. He was, however, an honourable man. And there were witnesses, plenty of them. He could not and did not tell them they had failed.

All he could reasonably do, if he could not bring himself to congratulate them on their betrothal, was to play for time. He reminded them again of what they faced. He alluded (according to those who told the story afterwards to Margaret) to the 'lewd words' (as Margaret called them) that Margery had chosen to add. These alone, he warned her, would be enough to bring down the lasting anger of her family. That can have been no news to Margery.

In view of the solemn nature of the situation, the bishop had decided to take soundings of others, learned men in the church and those who knew more about the couple and their situation. It might be that there was something he had overlooked, some factor that would inhibit a betrothal.

Can you not marry us now, Richard perhaps asked, if we swear to you that this is our choice, and we know of no impediment? We have waited a long time for this; we neither of us wish to wait any longer.

He could have done perhaps, but Bishop Lyhert was not the man to do that. When they pressed him, he gave them a date when he would pronounce his verdict, the Wednesday or Thursday after Michaelmas (the following week, most likely, or the one after). Then he dismissed them.

Ashfield had gone, so it was just with the servants as escort (servants who would not, on pain of their lives, have given her a chance to speak with Richard) that Margery went back to Princes Inn. The door was opened to her by Father Gloys.

You are not welcome here. You will never be welcome here again.

Then where am I to go, Margery must have asked? The bishop has not yet given his verdict. You know I cannot go to Richard's house.

That was the bishop's problem. Father Gloys did not dare to help her, and the Pastons had already sent out the word, he warned her, that they would take it amiss if any of their friends received her.

It must have been a strange anticlimax to have to retrace her steps to the bishop's palace, and to knock on the door, knowing that she was not expected this time. And even if the bishop felt some sympathy (he probably reckoned that however plainly he had put it, she had not taken it in before then what would happen), he cannot have liked to be landed with the problem of what to do with her. But there was little option but for him to tell his servants to do what was necessary. Messengers went out, soundings were taken, probably with Margaret Paston as well as with men and women who might be leaned upon to help.

It might have taken a while, but before nightfall Margery had been found temporary lodging. Roger Best, who had been lord mayor of Norwich a couple of years earlier, and his wife had agreed that they would put the girl up until the bishop's verdict came in. They were not close associates of the Pastons, and Margaret had indicated that she would not hold it against them if they assisted her daughter. It was a reasonable solution, she reckoned, since Best and his wife were noted for their 'sadness and good disposition'.[3] Margery would have no chance to meet with Richard while she was in their house, and would get plenty of lectures from Mistress Best in return for her supper.

Margery might have enjoyed the irony, but perhaps her mother did not even take it in. Roger Best was a grocer.

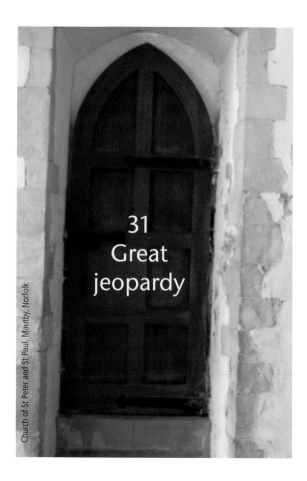

31
Great
jeopardy

Church of St Peter and St Paul, Mautby, Norfolk

Richard must have gone back to his own house. And like Margaret, he would have
learned what Margery had said. Someone would have told him too that she had been
denied the door at Princes Inn, and lodged with the Bests.

He probably took that hard. Whether the bishop had lectured Richard just as he
lectured Margery or not (quite possibly not, since even bishops talk differently to girls of
nineteen and to men of business in their thirties), he had known that the Pastons would
be angered if Margery did not deny him. But anger is one thing and disowning is another.
He had never intended to ruin Margery, and he, like she, must have believed that once
they had made their anger felt, her family would come round. This public rejection of her,
even before the bishop gave his verdict, made it likely if not certain that they would not.
If the bishop pronounced that the two were not validly betrothed she might possibly be
taken back into the household, but her life would be blighted beyond repair. If the bishop
confirmed that the betrothal was valid, her family might never speak to her again.

They might never speak to him either. This was no light matter, just as it was not
a cause for laughter that the bishop, whatever his motives, had painted him as a man
regarded as repugnant by Margery's family, her neighbours, her friends.

He knew he was not that. And he would recover somehow if he was turned off the
family's service (the duke of Norfolk would probably be glad to assist), but until this point
he might not ever have contemplated leaving the Pastons' employment.

The next few days would have been tense ones, and they were made more difficult still by the news that came from Caister. This too had looked from the start like an affair that could not end well, since there was not the remotest chance that the Pastons could match the duke of Norfolk's forces, and their resistance had intensified the duke's determination to take the place from them. Norfolk's lieutenant had ordered an assault, and done major damage to the castle. The word from its little garrison was confused and second hand, since none of the men had been able to get out to send a clear message.[1] But it was bad, indeed disastrous. John Daubeney was dead. It was rumoured another man, a relative of Margaret Paston's, had been killed too, and others of the small garrison were badly wounded. The men had run short of food, of gunpowder, of arrows. They had little option but to surrender, but the duke was so angry that they had fired on his men that it was by no means certain he would agree a truce and negotiate terms that would enable the remaining men to withdraw safely.

Daubeney dead. Killed in the cause of trying to keep for the Pastons a place that many, if not most, people believed the family had only acquired through fraud. They had all liked merry, brash John Daubeney. Richard had been his good friend, had worked with him for years. It must have put his own troubles into a harsh perspective. He might have been heartily glad he had not been at Caister when the duke's cannon began to fire, but at the same time he must have felt impotent and frustrated that he had been able to do nothing to save Daube.

It also made it very difficult for him to judge how to play the situation. This was a time when it would be callous to desert the Pastons, but how could he stay loyal in such circumstances? Was there a chance that if he did, they would swallow their pride and back down over the marriage? Might Margery take it as a betrayal if he continued to work for her family when she had been shut out by them?

Sir John sent to him, asking him to provide some money.[2] Richard must have thought hard what to do about that. Many men were owed money by the Pastons, and he himself was not the least of them. He had to consider his own interests,

Church of St Mary,
Shelton, Norfolk

and Margery's too. He did not reply, and did not send the money that was asked. For a while at least, Sir John would take it as a failure rather than a refusal.

He must have heard rumours, or more, that the Pastons were taking steps to secure their own position against him. Margaret had advised Sir John to send round to their estates, ordering men not to pay rents or the takings from crop sales over to Richard.[2] Richard had the deeds for some of their properties, and other papers that the family needed. They were considering, it appeared, how best to get these papers from him.

But only considering. It was a terrible time for the family leading up to the surrender of Caister, and little less terrible when the survivors limped out and left the place to the duke of Norfolk. It was apparent that food and arrows were not all they had lacked; some of the men had not had the inclination to risk their lives further in such a questionable cause. The Paston brothers must have been as drained as their men. Perhaps they did not have the determination at that point to take firm action on this other front and shut the door to Richard.

They had the ability still, he could not have doubted that. Even if Sir John was preoccupied elsewhere, his uncles were well practised in Paston grab and run tactics. If they had decided on action against him, he would have felt a firm hand on his neck. As yet, he had not.

At some point over these days he must have been visited by the bishop's men. The bishop himself probably did not confront him again, but he had plenty of willing intermediaries. Friends of Richard, or priests he knew well, would have sat down with him and asked him for his thoughts about the situation. They probably reminded him that the bishop had taken care to leave several paths open. An impediment could be found, and who better to discover it than Richard himself? Some at least of these intermediaries would have talked to Margaret Paston too, and called on the Bests and drank ale with Margery, with Mistress Best or her maid sitting by to make sure that all was done properly. They would have given Richard accounts – though not impartial ones – of what they had learned in these other quarters.

If he was tempted for a moment by these suggestions, it was probably no more than a moment. Whatever the bishop believed, it must have been evident to him that it had gone too far for any of them to retrace their steps. Anyway, he probably felt it would be dishonourable to draw back himself. If anyone did, it had to be Margery, but she had made her feelings clear, and whatever was hinted to him by the bishop's men, he can have had no sense that she had recanted.

Three things happened next. The bishop issued his verdict, Margery Paston left the Bests' house and went to stay at Blackborough nunnery, and Richard Calle called on Margaret Paston. They probably happened in that order, although since there is no dated record of the events, it is impossible to be sure.

Bishop Lyhert found in favour of the betrothal. Perhaps it was also a part of his pronouncement that the marriage between Margery Paston and Richard Calle should not take place immediately, but that Margery should spend some time – not a long time, but weeks rather than days – in the nunnery first. Or

both pictures, Church of St Mary, Martham, Norfolk

perhaps the Bests had thought better of their offer of hospitality, (they might have found Margery not nearly as repentant as they felt she ought to be) and she was sent to the nunnery because nowhere else could be found for her.

Richard might have waited till the verdict was known, and Margery was out of the city, before he headed to the Pastons' house.[4] If he did so; he might instead have met with Margaret on neutral ground, the home of a friend or the parlour of an inn. The meeting was probably his choice, not hers, but it could not have been easy for either of them.

Many letters flowed between the Paston men, and between them and their mother. There are none surviving from this time written by Richard himself, so what happened is not as clear as we might wish. But it seems that Richard decided it would be best to take the imitative himself, and spell out to the family how he wished things to take shape. They might then consider the situation for themselves without his further input, because he would not be staying in Norwich.

Richard can never have been in much doubt about the severity of the Pastons' financial crisis. It was worse now than ever, that was apparent. They had lost friends as well as land and property in standing up to the duke of Norfolk. The men who had been hired to guard Caister had been paid for their season of service – not generously, but fairly – and then let go; there was no need for them now. There was need for other men, but there was no money to pay them, or even to cover their keep. Seven men, including ones who had been in the family's service for years like John Pamping, would have to be turned off 'like masterless hounds'.[3] John III was casting around for other masters for them, and still hoped the Berneys might help, but it was no use turning to Margaret, although she had agreed to give them food and drink for a while, because she too was in such straits that she was facing the prospect of breaking up her own household.[6]

The Paston brothers could not pay Richard, and it was apparent too that there was enough bad blood between him and John III that it was not practicable for them to work together, as John III and his brother set about salvaging what they could from the remaining estates. For a while, he had no option but to withdraw from the family's service. But he had no wish to make this permanent. He must have believed there was still good will between him and some of the Pastons – William perhaps, even Sir John. The long years of work, the spell of imprisonment, the threats he had endured: he had no wish to wipe the slate of all this. So he told Margaret Paston that if in time Sir John felt able to take him back, then he would be willing to return. And until he had word from Sir John that this would not happen, he would commit himself to no new master.

He must have sent the same message direct to Sir John at much the same time.

He would turn over to them his books of account, and all of the papers he held that they might find useful. As for what he would do now, that was beyond questioning. He would go to Blackborough.

32

The fens in winter

Church of St Mary the Virgin, Wiggenhall, Norfolk

Blackborough nunnery was in Norfolk, but that is a large county, and the place was about as far from Norwich, Paston and Caister as it is possible to be within its confines. It was in the far west, in the low marshy land around the River Nar, which drains into the broad expanse of the Wash. There is much wetland in this area still, and in the fifteenth century there was a great deal more.

The nearest town is Middleton, a small one, but made more important because it was the seat of Lord Scales, one of the great landowners of West Norfolk. In the middle of the town there is still to be found the stumpy mound of the castle his ancestors built, with undulating ditches and earthworks surrounding it, and at the opposite side of the town from the nunnery – which was a mile or so distant from the old castle – was the huge red brick bulk of the newly built Middleton Castle in its moat.

The Pastons had had dealings for generations with Lord Scales, but then so had many people in the county. It was probably not to oblige them, but to oblige the bishop, that Margery was admitted to the nunnery that the Scales family had founded, and with which they were still closely involved.

Enough remains of the nunnery (though not much) to make it clear that it was built of carstone, the reddish stone that takes over in this area from the flint of the eastern parts of Norfolk. It was a Benedictine nunnery, not large: a century later the two courtyards sheltered nine professed nuns 'of good name and fame', a priest, eleven men servants and eight women servants.[1] The place was perhaps this size, or slightly bigger, when Margery was brought to it in the autumn of 1469.

She was not expected to take any vows; she came as a visitor. And she came either knowing that the bishop had cleared the way for her marriage, and that although she would soon be joined by Richard she might never see her family again, or guessing that this would be the news that followed her.

There are bleak October days and there are bright October days, so in the marshy lands by the Nar Margery probably saw both that autumn. Late in that year there was another comet, so perhaps she – and Richard, when he too had come to Blackborough – stood in the fields at Middleton and watched its arrow-shape forged in the sky.

Richard chatted with the nuns, and with Lord Scales' servants as well. He was a man with a gift for friendship, and these people had no cause to take him at John Paston III's estimation. Before long, he was putting the nunnery accounts in order and improving the collection system for its estates.[2]

This would not occupy him full time. When things settled down, he and Margery would head back east. He had his house in Norwich, and they had perhaps talked by now of getting a place in the country. The Pastons went rarely to Paston village, or to Bromholm Priory, where John senior's coffin still stood under its tattered pall of gold cloth. Both Richard and Margery must have loved the broad skies and flat fields of north-east Norfolk. Bacton or thereabouts would suit them well.

But this was in the future. The present was the quiet melancholy of all they had lost. And they had lost much, paid a higher price than they could ever have imagined when they first began to look at each other, and not look away. And the present was the joy, because their way was clear now.

They took it. At some time that winter, Margery Paston stood with Richard Calle, most likely in the doorway of Middleton Church, and they repeated the words that came after those they had already exchanged, those that bound them together in marriage.

This time, they had witnesses.

Both pictures, Church of St Peter, Ringland, Norfolk
Photos Mike Dixon

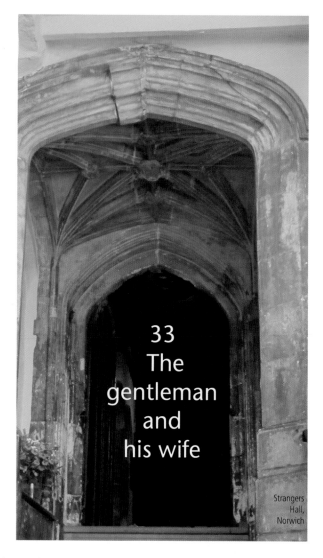

33
The gentleman and his wife

Strangers
Hall,
Norwich

It would be good to report that Richard and Margery lived a long and happy life together, but real life is not so kind. It might well have been a happy life they shared, but it was not a long one. Margery and Richard had three sons, whom they named John, William and Richard, but before the tenth anniversary of their marriage she was dead.[1]

Not long after their marriage Richard resumed work for the Paston family, and he continued to act as their chief land agent for a number of years.[2] The family had mixed fortunes over these years, and those beyond them. At one point a Paston became earl of Yarmouth, but later the family dwindled into the obscurity it had come from.

Margaret Paston was never reconciled with her daughter. Her grandchildren she must have warmed to, however, and when she died many years later, she left them small legacies in her will.

In time Richard married again and had further children. He seems still to have been alive in 1500, by which time he must have been a grey-haired man. He made his home in Bacton, the village next to Paston in Norfolk, in the shadow of Bromholm Priory, and within smelling distance of the North Sea. The papers that refer to him there designate him as 'Richard Calle, gentleman'.[3]

Church of St Mary, Shelton, Norfolk

Paston, Norfolk

Notes

Writing a book such as this would not be possible without the generations of scholars who have worked with the Paston letters and its other sources, and I owe a debt of gratitude to all of them.

The main source for this book is of course the Letters. I first became acquainted with James Gairdner's six-volume edition more than twenty years ago, and my first research made use of that. That has to a large extent been superseded by Norman Davis's majestic two-volume edition (in the original spelling, and with a third volume edited by Beadle and Richmond added in 2005), and I have given references to this where possible. I have also at times used a number of popular modern-language editions. The quotes in this book are in modernized spelling, and are my own (sometimes fairly approximate) renderings of the published documents in their original spelling.

Medieval letters are not a tidy resource. I have not consulted the originals, and where the editors of the editions I have used differ on dates or other details, I have used my own judgement. (Where that differs significantly from the opinion of others, it is noted below.) Similarly, different correspondents sometimes give accounts of incidents that do not readily match up, and I have judged in these cases what seems to best make sense.

On the few occasions where dialogue is given (and is not in inverted commas), it reflects the sense of a conversation related in more general terms in the letters.

No significant incidents have been invented, but I have done my best to construct a narrative that flows. Because the letters give a far from exhaustive account of events, the inevitable result is the frequent use of 'probably', 'possibly' and so on. I can only apologize if this becomes tedious, but I have tried not to introduce certainty where none exists in the sources. (The few occasions where I have guessed and not indicated that in the text are noted below.)

The other published and electronic sources I have consulted are given in the bibliography below. The notes are not intended to be exhaustive, but I hope that together with the bibliography, they will prove guidance sufficient for anyone wanting to know from where I have derived the material in this book. If readers wish to know more, I shall do my best to help: I can be contacted via lassepress@gmail.com

A note might be useful too on the illustrations. Of course, the East Anglia of today is very different from the region the Pastons and the Calles knew. Although some buildings survive from their era, they have often been much changed over the years, and even when it might at first glance appear natural, the landscape too has changed substantially. All the photographs are of East Anglia (or in a few cases London), but they are not all of the places where incidents in the book occurred; they are my attempt to give a sense of what such places might have been like. The stained glass too is from East Anglia, and from the information I have accessed (and my own judgement) is broadly contemporary with the events in the book, though much of this too has been repaired and reset over the centuries, so little of it looks exactly as it was when as the Pastons and their contemporaries saw it. Except where noted otherwise, the photographs are my own.

Norwich

G refers to Gairdner (1904) by volume (e.g. GV is volume 5); D refers to Davis (1971, 1976) similarly. References are to pages, not to numbered documents in these volumes. 'n' refers to a footnote in the source.

Chapter 1

1   Agnes's will (D1, 45–7) implies this was done on the judge's deathbed, but most likely it was agreed, if not implemented, on John and Margaret's marriage.
2   D1, lix, n. 18.
3   It seems to be broadly taken for granted by Paston scholars that John II and John III were Margaret's first two (surviving) children, and that Margery was born later, but there is no known date for Margery's birth. I've followed the usual assumption that Margery was born around 1450, but this does make her very young when her marriage first becomes a subject of discussion, so

    perhaps it should be regarded as open to doubt. She could not realistically have been born much later than this.
4   In D1, 45–6 Agnes Paston discusses her husband's will, but makes it clear that it was never finalized. (In fairness, she was convinced she had been told unambiguously of her husband's intentions; it was John Paston who refused to accept these were final.)
5   D1, 46.
6   The several mentions include D1, 233–4.

Chapter 2

1   Main sources for the incidents at Gresham are Margaret's letters no. 130 and 131 in D1 (pp. 226–30), John
    Paston's subsequent petition (D1, 51–3), and a letter from James Gloys (D2, 27–9).
2   Gloys is mentioned as drawing his dagger in D1, p. 224.
3   General information on Gresham is from Wikipedia and other sources (and from my own visits there). A keel of a boat was discovered when the castle moat was cleaned out in 1846.

4   Some writers on the Pastons, including Colin Richmond, have assumed the Pastons moved into the castle itself. But Partridge's men were in Gresham Castle, so logic says Margaret must have stayed somewhere else. Anyway, the house that can be demolished so easily (see below) does not sound like a stone castle, it sounds like a wood-framed country house.
5   Some think this a later legend – see e.g. http://www.norfolkcoast.co.uk/myths/ml_greshamgrasshopper.htm But it is probably an early one, revived later: see http://en.wikipedia.org/wiki/Thomas_Gresham
6   D2, 28.
7   Judging by the threat to kill John Damme along with John Paston, he must have given some support: see D1, 52.
8   D1, 226.
9   D1, 52.

Chapter 3

1   Among the sources for this is D1, 52.
2   We cannot be sure, because the Pastons did not document most of their children's births, and although Margaret's letters suggest sometimes that she was pregnant, it need not follow that she gave birth to a child that lived.
3   Sources for all these incidents include D1, 58–60.
4   D1, 76.

Chapter 4

1   All information on the Calle family comes from Romanes (1920). Details on the Calles in this period are scant, and I have made my best guess on the relationships between those who have left record, following Romanes.
2   He is often described as a bailiff, but I think this is misleading. A bailiff today is a low-level position, concerned largely with distraining goods from those in debt. Although this was a part of Richard's role, overall it involved much more

responsibility than a modern bailiff assumes. Estate manager and land agent are the most accurate contemporary terms.

3   D1, 116.

Chapter 5

1   D1, 231 gives Margaret's account of Agnes's help at this time.

2   Rye (1916). The Pastons rarely mention the location of their houses. Various historians of Norwich have claimed or speculated about them, not always convincingly. The most reliable source is information in wills of bequests to churches or of burials in them. There was also subsequently a public house called Princes Inn. See e.g. D1, 241, 246, 250.

3   From his draft will: D1, 148.

4   D1, 41.

5   D2, 32.

6   D1, 42. Lady Pole was perhaps the widow of a connection of the duke of Suffolk's.

Chapter 6

1   For assorted complaints against Judge Paston see D2, 508–15.

2   Virgoe (1988).

3   D1, 129.

4   D2, 333.

5   D2, 223–4. Davis dates to 'perhaps 1460', and thinks it was addressed to John II, not his father. I'm not convinced; it reads more as if it was written to John senior. Gairdner (GII, 187–8) thought it dated from November 1450, which would make it Richard's earliest surviving letter. Either way, it gives a good indication of the range of Richard's work.

6   D2, 113–14.

Chapter 7

1   The source for the Worcester quotes is Worcester (1969).

2   An example is D2, 109–10.

3   D1, 155 for William Paston's view of this.

4   Apparent in the many drafts of Fastolf's will, e.g. D1, 88.

Chapter 8

1   He had moved out for example by 1461, when Margaret Paston writes of his not being at home: D1, 274.

2   D1, 158.

3   Richmond (1996) is a detailed source on many aspects of this, see e.g. p. 69.

Chapter 9

1   See Richmond (1996), 71–2 for a summary of the funeral.

2   D2, 313–15.

3   D1, 257 details both sons' errands.

4   There were certainly a row, possibly at Fastolf's funeral. See e.g. D2, 332–5.

5   Some of this information is from Turner (1842). Modern Fastolf experts have found no independent corroboration of these details.

6   GII, 166–89. (There is also an inventory in D1, 107–14.)

Chapter 10

1   Main source for this incident is D2, 236–7.

2   D1, 392.

3   Richmond (1996), 107.

4   D2, 237.

5   D2, 237.

Chapter 11

1   D1, 267.

2   D1, 270.

3   D1, 266.

4   D1, 326.

5   Main sources for these events are Clement's letter, D1, 199–200, and John II's letter, D1, 390–3.

6   D1, 391.

Chapter 12

1   D1, 200–2.

2   D1, 201.

3   Margaret mentions a letter from John Calle in D1, 275.

4   D1, 270–1.

5   D2, 248.

6 D2, 247–9.

7 D2, 248.

8 D2, 253–5. This was probably the autumn of 1462, several months after Pamping's first efforts. Some of the letters dealing with these events were misdated by editors: see Richmond (2000), p. 199, n. 93, and Beadle and Richmond (2005), xxvi.

Chapter 13

1 Main source is D2, 369–71.

2 D2, 255.

3 D2, 370.

4 D2, 370–1.

5 D2, 257–8.

Chapter 14

1 D2, 293–4.

2 D1, 287.

3 D1, 388.

4 D2, 425.

Chapter 15

1 D1, 286–7.

2 Margaret writes 'my mother', but she usually refers in this way to Agnes Paston as well as to Margery Garneys, and here it would have been the former.

3 It is not clear from Margaret's account that there were several visitors, but I have assumed that was the case.

Chapter 16

1 D2, 348.

2 D2, 303.

3 D2, 304.

4 D1, 231.

5 D1, 210–14 for her will.

6 D1, 528.

7 See D2, 551 ff.

8 D1, 135.

Chapter 17

1 D1, 126–31 for letter; quote p. 129.

2 D1, 128.

3 See e.g. D1, 308, written shortly after this date.

4 D1, 296.

5 This account is adapted from the information in D1, 295–6.

6 D1, 295.

7 They did: it was Lypiate (D1, 300).

8 D2, 373.

Chapter 18

1 That she was living at least partly at Helesdon is clear from the inventory of goods taken, which includes her possessions: D1, 328.

2 Margaret's own term: D1, 298.

3 D2, 311.

4 D2, 310.

5 Richard writes that he was trapped at 'Swayne dore' (D2, 311). I cannot locate this precisely (perhaps it was the door of the Swayne family's house), but clearly it was in the city centre.

6 D2, 311.

7 D2, 312.

Chapter 19

1 Apparent from D1, 308.

2 D1, 145.

3 D1, 316.

4 Apparent from the account of the journey back, D1, 318–23.

5 D1, 528–9.

6 D1, 314.

7 D1, 529. Some commentators suggest the 'rood of Northedor' is a reference to Old St Paul's, and John might well have advised his mother and sister to admire its marvels, but there was a famous rood above the north door at Bermondsey – which John mentions particularly – and I can find no reference to one at St Paul's.

Chapter 20

1 D1, 318–22, and D1, 529–31.

2 D1, 531.

3 D1, 140–5.

Chapter 21

1 D1, 322.

2 D1, 324.
3 D1, 327.
4 D1, 324 and 330.
5 D1, 330.
6 D1, 324.
7 D1, 3326.
8 D1, 330.
9 D1, 326, 328.

Chapter 22

1 GIV, 226 ff has details of the funeral; I cannot locate the equivalent in Davis.
2 GIV, 231.
3 D1, 359.

Chapter 23

1 D1, 576.
2 D1, 334.
3 D1, 168.
4 D2, 586–90 (the college was Magdalen).
5 D2, 549–52.
6 D2, 392–3.

Chapter 24

1 D2, 392–3.

Chapter 25

1 Thomas Daverse, writing in 1467: D2, 379.
2 D2, 389–90.
3 We have John III's account of this meeting: D1, 541–2.

Chapter 26

1 D1, 538–40.
2 D2, 561–9 shows the change in his attitude.
3 Outlined e.g. in Virgoe (1989), 174.

Chapter 27

1 Various chroniclers mention the comet, e.g. Warkworth's chronicle in Chronicles of the White Rose (1845, 109).
2 D1, 398–9.

Chapter 28

1 D1, 339.
2 D1, 339.
3 D1, 336–8; quote on p. 336.
4 D1, 336.
5 D1, 543.
6 D1, 542.
7 D2, 395–7.

Chapter 29

1 D2, 498–500.

Chapter 30

1 The main source for all this chapter is D1, 341–4.
2 This account extrapolates a little from the information in Margaret's letter. For instance, it is not clear from Margaret's account exactly where Margery and Richard were examined: presumably in the cathedral precincts, probably not in the church itself. I've guessed at the bishop's chamber.
3 D1, 343.

Chapter 31

1 The main sources for this chapter are D1, 344–7, 406, 546, 559–60.
2 D1, 407.
3 D1, 413.
4 D1, 347. 'As it is told me', Margaret writes. I've taken it that she met with Richard, but arguably it was told to her at second hand.
5 John III's expression: D1, 547.
6 D1, 346–7.

Chapter 32

1 Details from British History Online. 'Houses of Benedictine nuns 12: the Priory of Blackborough.'
2 For Richard at Blackborough, D1, 549. As the nuns' receiver, Richmond (1990) p. 111 n. 200.

Chapter 33

1 Apparent from Margaret's will: D1, 388.
2 He was writing to the Pastons on business matters by 1472.
3 Details mostly from Romanes (1920).

Bibliography

Hard-copy publications

Armstrong, M. J. (1781) *History and Antiquities of the County of Norfolk. Vol. X: The City and County of Norwich.* Norwich: M. Booth.

Beadle, R. and Richmond. C. (2005) *Paston Letters and Papers of the Fifteenth Century, Part III.* Oxford: Oxford University Press for Early English Text Society.

Blomefield, Francis. (1806) *An Essay towards a Topographical History of the County of Norfolk. Vol. 3: The City and County of Norwich.* London: William Miller.

Britnell, R. H. (1988) 'The Pastons and their Norfolk', *Agricultural History Review* **36**(11), pp. 132–44.

Castor, Helen (2004) *Blood and Roses: The Paston family in the fifteenth century.* London: Faber & Faber.

Chronicles of the White Rose of York (1845) *The Chronicles of the White Rose of York: a series of historical fragments, proclamations, letters, and other contemporary documents relating to the reign of King Edward the Fourth.* London: James Bohn.

Coss, Peter (1998) *The Lady in Medieval England, 1000–1500,* Stroud, Glos.: Sutton.

Cuningham, W. (1559) Map of Norwich, between ff. 8–9 in *The Cosmographical Glasse, Conteinyng the Pleasant Principles of Cosmographie, Geographie, Hydrographie, or Nauigation.* London.

Davis, Norman (ed.) (1971) *Paston Letters and Papers of the Fifteenth Century, Part I.* Oxford: Oxford University Press.

Davis, Norman (ed.) (1976) *Paston Letters and Papers of the Fifteenth Century, Part II.* Oxford: Oxford University Press.

Davis, Norman (ed.) (1999) *The Paston Letters: A selection in modern spelling,* rev. pbk edn. Oxford: Oxford University Press.

Gairdner, James (1904) *The Paston Letters, a.d. 1422–1509, New complete library edition with notes and introduction.* 6 vols. London: Chatto & Windus/Exeter: James G. Commin.

Gilchrist, Robert and Oliva, Marilyn (1993) *Religious Women in Medieval East Anglia.* Studies in East Anglian History 1, Norwich: University of East Anglia Centre of East Anglian Studies.

Groves, Nicholas (2010) *The Medieval Churches of the City of Norwich.* Norwich: HEART and East Publishing.

Harvey, John H. (ed. and trans.) (1969) *William Worcester's Itineraries.* Oxford: Oxford University Press.

Hicks, Michael (1995) *Bastard Feudalism.* London and New York: Longman.

Higgins, Anne (1996) 'Work and plays: guild casting in the Corpus Christi drama', in L. Barroll (ed.), *Medieval and Renaissance Drama in England,* Vol. 7. Fairleigh Dickinson University Press.

Jeaffreson, J. C. (1873) *Brides and Bridals,* 2nd edn. London: Hurst & Blackett. Available at: www.archive.org/stream/bridesandbridal00jeafgoog#page/n6/mode/2up (accessed 14 March 2012).

Kelly, Serena, Rutledge, Elizabeth and Tillyard, Margot (1983) *Men of Property: An analysis of the Norwich enrolled deeds 1295–1311,* ed. Ursula Priestley. Norwich: University of East Anglia Centre of East Anglian Studies.

Leyser, Henrietta (1995) *Medieval Women: A social history of women in England 1450–1500.* London: Phoenix Press.

Lyle, Helen (1950) *The Rebellion of Jack Cade 1450.* London: Historical Association.

Macfarlane, Alan (1986) *Marriage and Love in England, 1300–1840.* Oxford: Blackwell.

Rawcliffe, Carole (1995) *The Hospitals of Medieval Norwich.* Studies in East Anglian History 2, Norwich: University of East Anglia Centre of East Anglian Studies.

Rawcliffe, Carole and Wilson, Richard (eds) (2004) *Medieval Norwich.* London and New York: Hambledon and London.

Richmond, Colin (1990) *The Paston Family in the Fifteenth Century, Vol. 1: The first phase.* Cambridge: Cambridge University Press.

Richmond, Colin (1996) *The Paston Family in the Fifteenth Century, Vol. 2: Fastolf's will* (pbk edn). Cambridge: Cambridge University Press.

Richmond, Colin (2000) *The Paston Family in the Fifteenth Century, Vol. 3: Endings.* Cambridge: Cambridge University Press.

Romanes, Charles S. (1920) *The Calls of Norfolk and Suffolk, their Paston Connections and Descendants,* privately printed, London.

Rowling, Marjorie A. (1989) 'New evidence on the disseisin of the Pastons from their Norfolk manor of Gresham, 1448–1451.' *Norfolk Archaeology,* vol. 40, pp. 302–8.

Rye, Walter (1916) *Norwich Houses before 1600,* privately printed.

Sayer, Michael (1977) 'Norfolk involvement in dynastic conflict 1469–71 and 1483–87', *Norfolk Archaeology* 36(iv), 305–26.

Smith, Anthony (1995) '"The greatest man of that age": the acquisition of Sir John Fastolf's East Anglian estates', in Rowena E. Archer and Simon Walker (eds), *Rulers and Ruled in Late Medieval England: Essays presented to Gerald Harriss.* London and Rio Grande: Hambledon Press.

Turner, Dawson (1842) *Sketch of the History of Caister Castle, nr. Yarmouth.* Whittaker.

Virgoe, Roger (1988) 'A Norwich taxation list of 1451', *Norfolk Archaeology* **40**(2), pp. 145–54.
Virgoe, Roger (ed.) (1989) *Illustrated Letters of the Paston Family*, London: Macmillan.
Watt, D. (2004) *The Paston Women: Selected letters, translated from the Middle English with introduction, notes and interpretive essay*. Cambridge: D. S. Brewer.
White, Francis (1854) *Francis White's History, Gazetteer and Directory of Norfolk 1854*, pp. 664–5. Available on: http://apling.freeservers.com/Villages/Middleton54.htm (accessed 26 February 2012).
Williamson, Tom (2006) *England's Landscape: East Anglia*. London: Collins.
Wolgar, Christopher (1995) 'Diet and consumption in gentry and noble households: a case study from around the Wash', in Rowena E. Archer and Simon Walker (eds), *Rulers and Ruled in Late Medieval England: Essays presented to Gerald Harriss*. London and Rio Grande: Hambledon Press.
Worcester, William (1969) *Itineraries*, ed. and trans. J. Harvey. Oxford: Clarendon Press.

Electronic sources

Bethancourt ,W. J. III. 'The form of matrimony in the European Middle Ages as reconstructed by W. J. Bethancourt III.' www.dfwx.com/medieval.html (accessed 14 March 2012).
British History Online. 'Houses of Benedictine nuns 12: the Priory of Blackborough.' www.british-history.ac.uk/report.aspx?compid=38269 (accessed 26 February 2012).
British History Online 'Houses of Cluniac monks 18: the Priory of Bromholm.' www.british-history.ac.uk/report.aspx?compid=38275 (accessed 26 February 2012).
British Listed Buildings. 'Cotton Hall, Cotton, Suffolk' http://www.britishlisted buildings.co.uk/en-281599-cotton-hall-cotton-suffolk (accessed 15 February 2013).
British Listed Buildings. 'Hempnalls Hall, Cotton, Suffolk' http://www.britishlistedbuildings. co.uk/en-281611-hempnalls-hall-cotton-suffolk (accessed 15 February 2013).
Framlingham. Framlingham town trail. www.framlingham.com/documents/trailMap.pdf; www. framlingham.com/documents/FramlinghamTownTrail.pdf (accessed 4 March 2012).
Gatehouse Record. 'Drayton Old Lodge.' http://homepage.mac.com/philipdavis/English% 20sites/1950.html (accessed 4 March 2012).
Great Waldingfield. Viillage website. www.greatwaldingfield.co.uk/home.html (accessed 4 March 2012).
Halhed family genealogy. www.halhed.com/t4r/getperson.php?personID=I4257&tree=tree1 (accessed 21 January 2012).
Knott, Simon. 'St Clement Conesford.' www.norfolkchurches.co.uk/norwichclementconesford/ norwichclementconesford.htm (accessed 26 February 2012).
Literary Norfolk. www.literarynorfolk.co.uk/mautby.htm (accessed 26 February 2012).
Michalove, Sharon. 'Bibliographies: marriage in fifteenth-century England: Part II, secondary sources.' www.the-orb.net/bibliographies/marriag2.html (accessed 21 January 2012).
Michalove, Sharon. 'The great marriage hunt: finding a wife in fifteenth-century England.' http://history.eserver.org/finding-a-wife.txt (accessed 26 February 2012).
Mullini, Roberta. 'Tradition and innovation in the Paston women's "ego-documents".' www. women.it/cyberarchive/files/mullini.htm (accessed 26 February 2012).
Norwich Blackfriars. 'Medieval Norwich.' www.norwichblackfriars.co.uk/medieval-norwich-2/ (accessed 4 March 2012).
Norwich Churches. 'St Peter Hungate.' www.norwich-churches.org/St%20Peter%20Hungate/ home.shtm (accessed 7 September 2012).
Ohlgren, Thomas H. 'Richard Call, the Pastons, and the manuscript context of "*Robin Hood and the Potter*" (Cambridge, University Library Ee.4.35.1).' http://web.ics. purdue.edu/~ohlgren/RobinHood/Paston.htm (accessed 21 January 2012).
Paston Research Group. 'The Paston family in Elm Hill: findings of the Paston Research

Group.' www.hungate.org.uk/Downloads/The-Pastons-Family-in-Elm-Hill.aspx (accessed 26 February 2012).

Searle, Eleanor M. (1981) 'Women and marriage in medieval society.' http://calteches.library. caltech.edu/583/2/Searle.pdf (accessed 14 March 2012).

Trytel. 'Corbridge map' picture of St Peter Hungate, Norwich. http://users.trytel.com/tristan/ towns/florilegium/popreli01.html for (accessed 26 February 2012).

Tudorplace 'The Pastons' (for information mostly on Richard Calle). www.tudorplace.com.ar/PAS-TON.htm (accessed 21 January 2012).

Wikipedia. 'Bromholm Priory, Norfolk' (accessed 26 February 2012).

Wikipedia. 'Gresham Castle' (accessed 19 July 2012).

Wikipedia. 'Gresham, Norfolk' (accessed 26 February 2012).

Wikipedia. 'List of monastic houses in Norfolk' (accessed 26 February 2012).

Wikipedia. 'Mautby, Norfolk' (accessed 26 February 2012).

Wikipedia. 'Paston, Norfolk' (accessed 26 February 2012).

Wikipedia. 'Robert Hungerford, Lord Moleyns' http://en.wikipedia.org/wiki/Robert_ Hungerford,_Lord_Moleyns (accessed 4 March 2012).

Church of St Mary, Shelton, Norfolk

Acknowledgements

Particular thanks are due to:

- my husband Paul Simmonds, who has visited all too many churches and castles with me, read and commented on successive drafts, and proofread the book for me
- Chris Carr, who accompanied me on several research trips, and read a draft and provided detailed and extremely useful comments
- other readers of the book in draft form: Rose Graham, Colin Richmond, Peter Wenban, Elizabeth-Anne Wheal
- Mike Dixon, for permission to use the photos on page 161.

adapted from a brass at the Church of St Margaret, Ormesby, Norfolk

General index

Note: nobles are indexed under their titles, not under family names. Notes are referenced as e.g. 166n1-2 for the second note for chapter 1 on p. 166.

A

agriculture *see* farming
Arnold, Davy, 116
Ashfield, Master, 152–4

B

Bacon family, 6–7
Bacon, Sir Edmund, 9
Baconsthorpe, Norfolk, 13
Bacton, John, 5, 31, 32
Bacton, Norfolk, 161, 163
    see also Bromholm Priory
bailiff *see* land agent
Beaufort, Lady Anne, 125
bedeman, 36, 58
Bedford, duchess of, 143–4
Berney family, 3, 5–6, 8, 159
Berney, John, 11–12
Berney, Philip, 16
Best, Roger (and wife), 155, 158–9
Blackborough nunnery, Norfolk, 158–9, 160–1
Bond, Thomas, 86
bonded status, 6, 10, 90, 125
Bottesford, Master, 113, 115
brewing, 62–3, 78, 98
Bromholm Priory, 27, 119–21, 163

C

Cade, Jack, rebellion of, 15, 16, 48–
Caister, Norfolk
    Castle, 38–40, 48, 51–2, 75, 119; duke of Norfolk's occupations 54–5, 57, 59, 60, 68–9; Pastons at, 51–2, 60, 94, 124, 133, 141, 144; sale to duke of Norfolk, 55–6, 138; siege of, 150–1, 157–8
    college of monks, 41, 44, 46, 48, 51, 62, 69, 77, 92–3; relocated, 125
    Roman ruins, 39–40
Calcott, Suffolk, 77, 110–11
Calle family, 18–20, 54, 104, 166–7n4-1
    family tree, 22
    history, 1, 18, 19
    lands and possessions, 18, 19
    relations with dukes of Norfolk, 20, 54–5, 57, 69, 75, 78, 140, 144
    social position, 32, 74, 135, 162
    see also individual family members by name
Calle, John (brother of Richard), 18, 54–5, 57, 69, 75, 87, 90–1, 104, 130

Calle, Richard, 18–21, 31–6, 43–6, 54–9, 66–72, 74–7, 81, 90–1, 92–6, 104, 107, 110–12, 113–17, 122–3, 126–30, 139, 144–5, 156–9
    attack on and threats against, 100–1
    at Blackborough, 161
    character, 20, 32–3, 43–4, 96, 126, 128–9, 139, 141, 159, 161
    children of, 162
    choice of profession, 20–1
    at Caister, 40–1
    at Cotton, 71–2, 74, 77, 110–12
    courtship and marriage, 1, 44, 126–30, 132–5, 139–42, 146–8, 154–5, 158, 161, 162
    early career, 20–1, 31–6
    education, 19–20
    family, 18–20 (*see also* Calle family)
    finances, 126, 129
    in Framlingham, 19, 54–9
    friends and acquaintances, 35, 40, 44, 75–6, 129, 134, 161
    at Hellesdon, 62, 94–6, 98, 114
    homes, 43, 126, 161, 163
    imprisoned, 74–7
    journeys to/from London, 32, 104, 110–11, 122, 132, 145
    letters of, v, 32, 35–6, 57–9, 76–8, 101, 141–2, 146–8, 167n6-5
    letters written for others, 32, 44
    in Norwich, 43, 100–1, 107, 113, 116, 122, 154–5, 156–9, 168n18-5
    poem about, 112
    possessions, 114, 117, 129
    relations with John Paston sr, 34, 36, 75–8, 91, 101
    relations with Margaret Paston, 34, 44, 95, 110, 133, 145, 148, 158–9, 169–70n31-4
    relations with other Paston family members, 66, 76, 81, 101, 122–3, 132–3, 144, 156–9
    resumes work for Pastons, 162
    servants of, 43–4, 123, 148
    summonses against, 74–5, 76, 77, 86, 99
    wages in arrears, 119, 126, 129, 145, 157–9
    withdrawal from Pastons' service, 156, 159
    work for Pastons, 1, 31–5, 40–1, 44, 45–9, 63, 66–72, 74–8, 90, 99–101, 107, 110–12, 113–14, 116–17, 122–3, 126, 129, 136, 145, 157–8, 167n4-2
    work other than for the Pastons, 32, 35, 126, 161
Calle, Simon (father of Richard), 18, 19, 54
Canterbury, archbishop of, 72
Castillon, battle of, 16
Catherine of Valois, queen of England, 109
Cawston, Norfolk, 98

Index of illustrations

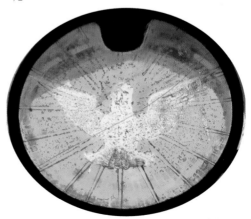

Church of St Mary, Saxlingham Nethergate, Norfolk

Also by Susan Curran and published by the Lasse Press

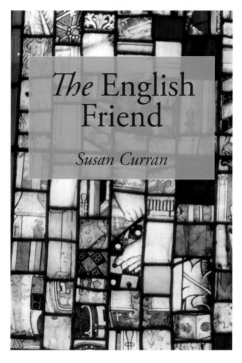

An illustrated biography of William de la Pole, first duke of Suffolk (1396–1450)

William de la Pole spent half his life fighting for the Lancastrian kings in France, in the later stages of the Hundred Years War. The war cost him his father and his four brothers. Taken prisoner, he lost a fortune paying his ransom – and gained two friends: his captor, the bastard of Orleans, and the bastard's half-brother, the famous French poet Charles of Orleans. Suffolk, also a poet, was to become Orleans' jailer. He spent the remainder of his life trying to bring about peace between England and France. It made him the most hated man in England.

This powerful true story of friendship, loyalty and treachery is the first full-length biography of an extraordinary man. Susan Curran uses a wide range of sources including contemporary documents and chronicles to bring Suffolk's story to life. The illustrations include photographs of the places Suffolk knew, and many stunning examples of contemporary stained glass from England and France.

First published 2011.
ISBN -13: 978-0-9568758-0-8 (large-format paperback)
Also available in a range of electronic editions.

For more information on all Lasse Press books, visit

www.lassepress.com